ANXIETY IN RELATIONSHIP

Stop Worrying and Overthinking. Understand the Causes of Stress of Your Couple and Finally Overcome Conflicts, Jealously and Insecurity

Isabella Gray

Table of contents

Introduction

When either or more parties in the partnership invest more time worrying more about relationships anxiously than tend to the partnership itself, it is recognized in the relationship as anxiety or you have anxiety in relationship. Fears may change, but the unpleasant problems remain the same. Fear of rejection, unceasing anxiety over infidelity, acting as though they value more, or an overwhelming fear of the viability of the partnership results in a loss of faith. There are several factors why you may experience distress in partnerships. Anxiety may be triggered by nervous ties to poisonous exes, parents, inadequate contact, and as causes, bad guidance. For e.g., partnership self-help books will also promote remote, enigmatic, and ambiguous actions to hold a spouse hooked, but neither of these aspects cultivate a strong relationship of confidence. There is not always an untrustworthy companion for individual experiencing anxiety in a relationship. Because if you don't communicate your worries and needs, you might very well be living your life, utterly oblivious of your problems. Around the same time, unrest is encouraged by every action that leads one partner to doubt the other. Anxiety can spike from secretive communications, nano-cheating, messages, and not connecting with your spouse.

Similarly, when you don't feel your best and most safe, your anxiety could skyrocket. Social networking just doesn't help. In reality, when contrasting partnerships on social networking sites, relationship anxiety bursts. The game of comparison and contrast encourages anxiety that your partnership is not as good as others, which allows nervous thoughts to grow as you ruminate on why your partnership is not as good as others, which, of course, is all projection.

Holding a sense of self apart from partner is important. Having a carrot cake and it's not a smoothie should be the target for a partnership. In other terms, in order to be integrated into a pair, we cannot forego important pieces of who we are. Rather than, each one of us, even as we step closer, can work to preserve the special facets of our own selves that drew us to one another in the same place. Of us should hold firm in this manner, realizing such that we are an actual being in and of themselves. In terms of age and the kindness shared, a partnership should be fair. We should easily express what we want if stuff seems wrong, but we do not ask our spouse to read our thoughts or know precisely what to do every time. It is a complicated loop from which to crack free as early as we are in the blame game. That's how you should deal with uncertainty regarding your friendship.

Chapter 01: Understanding Anxiety

This chapter explains an understanding of recognizing your anxiety in all perspectives. You can also get the idea that how to recognize and cancel your anxiety triggers. Some possible causes of anxiety and its common symptoms are also addressed. How to know the signs of anxiety and some natural remedies of chronic anxiety that you have never heard, all aspects are discussed in detail in a given chapter below.

1.1 Recognizing anxiety

Anxiety is the physiological reaction of the body to stress. It is a sense of fear or uncertainty of what is to come. Many individuals may feel afraid and insecure for the very first day of their school, or going to a work interview, or delivering a speech. But you might have an anxiety disorder if the symptoms of anxiety are severe, persist for more than 6 months, and interfere with life.

Anxiety disorders:

Feeling nervous about shifting to a new place, beginning a new career, or taking a test is common. This sort of anxiety is stressful, but it will inspire you to do a better job and to work harder. A sensation that ebbs and flows, but does not conflict with the daily existence, is ordinary anxiety.

The sense of dread can always be with you in the event of an anxiety disorder. It is severe and exhausting often. This kind of anxiety will lead you to avoid doing activities that you love. It can prohibit you from using an elevator, exiting your house, or even crossing a road, in serious situations. The fear will keep becoming stronger if left unchecked.

The most popular type of mental illness is an anxiety disorder which may influence someone at any age. Women tend to be recognized with an anxiety condition than males, according to APA.

Types of anxiety disorders:

Anxiety is a key aspect in many various conditions. They include:

- Panic disorder: at unpredictable moments, having recurrent panic attacks. In fear of the next panic attack, a person which has panic disorder may live.
- Disorder of social anxiety: intense fear of being criticized in social settings by others
- (PTSD) Post-traumatic stress disorder: trauma during a stressful experience
- Phobia: intense fear of a single entity, circumstance, or behavior
- Obsessive-compulsive disorder: repetitive unreasonable feelings that cause you to commit specific actions that are repeated
- Illness paranoia disorder: anxiety (formerly named hypochondria) concerning your well-being
- Separation anxiety disorder: anxiety of being separated from loved ones or homes.

Anxiety symptoms:

Depending on the individual feeling it, anxiety seems distinct. Feelings can vary from increasing heartbeat to butterflies in the stomach. You could feel out of balance like your body and mind are detached. Nightmares, panic attacks, painful feelings, or memories that can't be handled are some aspects that people feel fear. You might have a general sense of fear and concern, or you may be scared of a particular location or occurrence.

- General fear may include:
- Higher heart rate
- Difficulty in falling asleep
- Restlessness
- Fast breathing
- Trouble attention

Your signs of anxiety may be entirely different from everyone else. That's why understanding all the forms that anxiety may show itself is important. You may learn about the different kinds of signs of anxiety that you could feel.

Knowing an anxiety attack:

A sensation of intense apprehension, discomfort, concern, or fear is an anxiety attack. An anxiety attack occurs gradually for certain persons. When a traumatic occurrence approaches, it can worsen.

Anxiety disorders may differ widely, and effects can differ between persons. That is because not everyone feels the many signs of anxiety, and they can evolve over time. Symptoms of anxiety problem that are typical include:

- Feeling dizzy or faint
- Dry mouth
- breathing difficulty
- Sweating
- Worry and apprehension
- Hot flashes or chills
- Restlessness
- Fear
- Distress
- Tingling or numbness

There are several similar signs that a panic disorder and an anxiety episode share, but they are not the same.

Causes of anxiety:

Researchers really are not aware of the specific cause of anxiety. But, a variety of factors is likely to play a part. These involve environmental or genetics influences and can also Include brain chemistry.

Furthermore, researchers suggest that the regions of the brain which is responsible for anxiety regulation may be involved. The present study into anxiety provides a more in-depth look at the areas of the brain implicated in anxiety.

Tests that can diagnose anxiety:

You can't detect anxiety with a single test. Instead, a diagnosis of fear involves a long period involving psychological questionnaires, physical examinations, and mental health evaluations. Some doctors can perform a physical examination to rule out medical conditions that are underlying that may lead to the symptoms you encounter, including urine or blood tests. To help the doctor determine the amount of distress that you are feeling, some anxiety tests and measures are often included.

Treatments for anxiety:

You should discuss therapeutic strategies with your psychiatrist after you have been identified with anxiety. Medical treatment isn't appropriate for certain individuals. To help with the signs, lifestyle changes could be enough. However, in mild to extreme situations, treatment will help you conquer the symptoms and have a regular life that is more manageable.

Anxiety treatment consists of two parts: medications and psychotherapy. Meeting with a psychologist or therapist will help you develop techniques to use when it arises and methods to deal with anxiety. To treat anxiety, drugs contain sedatives and antidepressants. They work to stabilize the physiology of the brain, eliminate anxiety attacks, and ward off the more serious symptoms of the problem.

Natural remedies for anxiety:

Changes in lifestyles can be an efficient way to relieve any of the anxiety and tension that you can deal with every day. Many of the natural treatments are to take care of the body, remove harmful ones, and take part in safe practices.

They include:

- Having sufficient sleep
- Quit caffeine
- Remaining busy and exercise
- Meditate

- Eating a balanced diet
- Alcohol prevention
- remain healthy and work out
- quitting tobacco smoking

Helping children with anxiety:

Anxiety is common and natural in children. One in eight kids, in reality, may feel anxiety. They usually build strategies to control themselves and deal with feelings of fear as kids grow and learn from parents, classmates, and caretakers.

Although, fear may often become persistent and chronic in adolescents, evolving into an anxiety disorder. This uncontrolled anxiety can start to interfere with everyday tasks, and children can stop communicating with their friends or members of the family. Anxiety disorder symptoms could be:

- Insomnia
- Jitteriness
- Irritability
- Feelings of anxiety
- Feeling of isolation
- Shame

- Cognitive-behavioral therapy (CBT) or talk therapy and drugs provide anxiety counseling for children.

Helping teens with anxiety:

There could be many reasons for teenagers to be anxious. In these crucial years, exams, first dates, and college all pop up. Yet in teenagers who feel nervous or regularly develop anxiety symptoms may lead to an anxiety disorder.

Nervousness, shyness, avoidance, and isolation behavior can be signs of anxiety in adolescents. Similarly, anxiety in adolescents may relate to odd behaviors. They will act out, do poorly in school, neglect social interactions, and even indulge in drug or alcohol usage.

Anxiety and the use of alcohol:

If you are constantly nervous or anxious, you may decide that you would like a drink to relax your nerves. Alcohol is a sedative, after all. It will depress the central nervous system's function, which will make you feel more comfortable. That might sound like just the solution you want to let down your guard in a social environment. It might not, necessarily, be the right option. In an attempt to feel better on a daily basis, certain persons with anxiety disorders wind up consuming alcohol or other substances. This will build addiction and dependence. Treating alcohol or opioid addiction might be important until anxiety can be treated. Eventually, prolonged or long-term usage will cause the disorder worse, too.

Anxiety and its relation with depression:

You might even be depressed if you do have an anxiety

disorder. While depression and anxiety may appear independently, it is not uncommon for mental health conditions to appear together. A sign of clinical or severe depression maybe anxiety. Similarly, deteriorating depressive symptoms may be induced by an anxiety disorder. With several of the same therapies, the effects of both disorders may be managed: psychotherapy or counseling, medicines, and improvements in lifestyle.

Anxiety and its relation with stress:

Anxiety and stress are two sides of a coin. The result of burdens on your body or brain is stress. It may be the product of an occurrence or behavior that makes you uncomfortable or upset. Anxiety is the same type of terror, apprehension, or unease. Anxiety may be a response to stress, but in individuals who do not have visible stressors, it may also arise. Physical and emotional effects are triggered by both stress and anxiety. They include:

- Headaches

- Increase heartbeat
- Stomach pain
- Transpiration
- The Dizziness
- Tension in the muscles
- Jitteriness
- Rapid respiration
- Feeling nervous
- Panic
- Trouble focusing
- Restlessness
- Sleeplessness
- Rage or irritability that is unreasonable

Neither anxiety nor stress is always evil. In reality, each will provide you with a little boost or motivation to complete the mission or goal before you. They will, though, begin to mess with your everyday life if they become chronic. It is indeed necessary to get help in that situation. Chronic health conditions, including cardiac failure, are found in the long-term potential for chronic anxiety and depression. You should always understand that why there are anxiety and stress and how the problems can be handled.

Risk factors and causes of anxiety:

It is important to remember that everyone experiences anxiety frequently in their lives to a degree. Fear and anxiety are positive feelings that will serve to help us recognize hazards or challenges that keep us healthy and help us adjust to our environment. Anxiety disorders arise when the capacity to cope in essential aspects of life, such as education, job, or relationships, is impaired by extreme anxiety. There are several common risk factors for anxiety disorders, and many different combinations of predisposing factors are likely to be encountered by most individuals, such as neuro-biological influences, environmental influences, genetic variants, and life experiences. We may not yet completely comprehend what triggers certain persons to develop anxiety disorders, though.

Comorbidity is more associated with anxiety disorders than not, meaning that several separate forms of anxiety are encountered by most people who suffer significant anxiety. It is not shocking, considering this comorbidity, that certain risk factors are associated with anxiety disorders, or have the same underlying triggers. There is a great deal of research that examines risk factors for anxiety disorders and this analysis shows that both nurture and nature are very significant. It should be found out that no particular potential risk is definitive. Some patients will have a risk factor of a disorder and the disorder might not actually occur. Nevertheless, it is useful for studies to recognize risk factors and for individuals to be conscious of them. Being aware of others could be at risk will possibly help persons seek help or support to avoid a disorder from emerging.

Demographic characteristics influence anxiety disorders risks as well. Although there is no clear agreement, research shows that the risk of anxiety disorders declines over the lifetime, and later in life lower risk is seen. Women are much more likely to suffer from anxiety disorders. Gender, since females are twice as likely to suffer from anxiety as males, is another significant socio-demographic and biological anxiety disorder risk factor. Compared to males, average symptom severity in women has often been found to be more severe, and women who have anxiety disorders normally experience a poorer quality of life than males. This sex differential is not unique to anxiety disorders in the severity and prevalence of anxiety disorders which place women at risk over men but is often seen in depression and other adverse health effects (i.e., obesity and cardio-metabolic disease) due to stress. Studies show that ovarian hormones such as progesterone and estrogen and their fluctuations can play a significant role in the severity and prevalence of this gender variation in anxiety disorder. Although increases in progesterone and estrogen are associated with a difference in the magnitude of anxiety symptoms over the month and also across the lifespan and have been found to influence systems involved in the cause of anxiety disorders (i.e. the stress axis), it is uncertain if these hormones and the variations improve the sensitivity of women to anxiety.

Genetic risk factors for every anxiety disorder have been documented. Studies suggest that rates of heritability for anxiety disorders vary from 30-67%. Many experiments have concentrated on finding particular genetic causes that raise one's likelihood of an anxiety disorder, both historical and current. To date, a variety of single (nucleotide polymorphisms) SNPs or minor genetic code variants that confer an elevated risk of anxiety have been identified. For the most part, inside genes that are important for the development and control of stress hormones or neurotransmitter systems, the variants correlated with concern for anxiety are found.

it is important to remember that genetic factors may also provide resistance to anxiety disorders and large scale genomics studies continue to be performed in the field to find novel genetic factors associated with the anxiety disorders in the hope of better perspective biological mechanisms that 1) leads to the maintenance and development of anxiety; 2) can lead to improved treatment for such disorders. Most patients are not informed of the particular genetic markers they might have that impart chance for anxiety disorders, but if a person has a past of anxiety disorders within their family, there is an easy way to measure genetic risk. Although both nature and environment may be at play in family history, genetic susceptibility to anxiety possibly resides in the family if many persons have anxiety disorders.

Experiencing a persistent medical disease or a serious or recurrent injury may often raise the likelihood of anxiety disorders, and also the care of a family member and loved one with a severe illness. In several circumstances, a physician can conduct physical tests to rule out underlying medical disorders, provided that many health issues have been related to severe anxiety. Thyroid disease, for example, is also described by having severe anxiety symptoms. Anxiety disorders have also been correlated with menopause, heart failure, and diabetes. In addition, substance addiction or removal of certain medications is marked by acute or intense anxiety, and the likelihood of experiencing an anxiety condition may be elevated by persistent drug abuse. Anxiety can also occur as a side effect of some medications. A risk factor for having an anxiety disorder might still be having severe sleep problems, such as remaining asleep or trouble falling asleep.

Parenting behavior may also influence the potential for anxiety

problems with respect to environmental conditions within the family. The occurrence of anxiety disorders has been linked with parents who exhibit a strong degree of influence (as opposed to giving children autonomy) when communicating with children. Parental modeling of nervous symptoms and the child's parental disapproval has since been found to actually be correlated with a greater likelihood of anxiety. The occurrence of anxiety disorders is often correlated with enduring traumatic life experiences or persistent stress. The likelihood of developing anxiety disorders later in life may be enhanced by traumatic life experiences in adolescence, including hardship, physical, sexual or emotional violence, or parental loss or separation. Having witnessed a traumatic incident or a rather upsetting situation may be a contributing factor across all age ranges for the occurrence of anxiety. This is often proposed to contribute to elevated risk in line with the idea of chronic life tension resulting in greater anxiety risk, getting poorer access to social services, or becoming a part of a minority community.

The risk may also be greatly influenced by lifestyle habits, as heavy use of nicotine or caffeine may raise anxiety, whereas daily activity may reduce anxiety. There could also be a chance of developing an anxiety condition with particular temperament and attitude features. The likelihood of experiencing an anxiety condition later in life may be raised with respect to temperament, shyness, and behavioral avoidance in childhood. The Five-Factor Personality Model comprises of five large attribute domains, namely Openness to Experience, Extraversion, Neuroticism, Agreeability, and Conscientiousness, about personality characteristics. There is a greater probability for all psychological problems towards a person elevated on neuroticism trait or low on conscientiousness trait, while a person low on extraversion trait is at a higher risk of experiencing agoraphobia and social phobia. It has also been noticed that certain more limited personality traits contribute to anxiety risk, including a negative or aggressive attributional style, sensitivity to fear, and self-criticism. It has also been found that behavioral problems contribute to an elevated incidence of anxiety disorders.

Relation of anxiety and physical health:

Anxiety disorders raise the risk of suffering from many other physical illnesses, such as heart disease, cardiovascular disorders, like obesity, and diabetes. More importantly, anxiety has been related to high blood pressure, increased body weight and abdominal fat, and higher levels of cholesterol, triglycerides, and glucose. Although it is still uncertain what triggers the elevated co-morbidity of anxiety and negative performance in physical health, evidence indicates that improvements in anxiety-characteristic underlying biology can also promote the emergence over time of certain other physical health-related outcomes. Changes in the autonomic reactions, stress hormones, and elevated systemic inflammation, for instance, are all related to negative health effects and anxiety disorders. These mutual physiological conditions mean that they have common fundamental physiology and also that anxiety may be a disease of the entire body.

Chronic stress in life is linked with anxiety disorders. The cardiovascular system and stress hormone system is continuously activated by unresolvable, uncertain, unrelenting stressors that contribute to states of continuous increased activity. Biologically, because of constant stressors, the body has adapted to cope with immediate and unique threats in the environment. Exposure to an immediate danger stimulates the ANS (autonomic nervous system), i.e., elevated adrenaline levels and rapid breathing, and increasing heart rate, in normal circumstances in which chronic stress is low. In exchange, these responses induce stress hormones, like cortisol, to trigger. In order to respond to the immediate danger, one of the actions of such stress hormones is to raise glucose levels in the blood such that muscles can be triggered for flight or battle response. As mechanisms such as repairing and healing will delay until after the danger subsides, another role of stress hormones is to weaken the immune system. However, the stress hormone mechanism lacks the capacity to regulate immune function in someone with anxiety disorders, where certain reactions to daily stressors are continuously triggered, thereby leading to increased systemic inflammation that raises the likelihood of cardiovascular and autoimmune disorders. In the hope of discovering potential treatments that will relieve distress and prevent the progression of these whole-body conditions, clinical research and neuroscience begin to explore how anxiety disorders raise the human likelihood of experiencing co-morbidities in physical health.

1.2 How to recognize and cancel anxiety triggers?

Anxiety is a state of mental condition that may cause feelings of worry, fear, or tension. Anxiety may also cause heart problems and severe physical effects for certain persons, such as chest pain. There are extremely prevalent anxiety conditions. According to a survey, they impact an estimated 40 million individuals in the US.

What induces conditions like anxiety or anxiety disorder may be confusing. A combination of variables, including biology and environmental conditions, are likely to play a part. It is obvious, however, that some activities, experiences, or emotions can start or make them worse, triggering symptoms of anxiety. These factors are considered as triggers

For each individual, anxiety triggers may be different, but for individuals with these disorders, certain triggers are similar. Many persons feel that they have several causes. But for certain persons, for no cause at all, anxiety disorders may be caused. It's necessary to uncover any anxiety causes you might have, for that reason. A significant phase in handling them is knowing the causes.

Basic anxiety triggers:

The following are some of the more popular causes that can trigger anxiety in any person:

Conflict can cause anxiety:

Problems with relationships, arguments, disagreements, any of these problems can trigger or intensify anxiety. If you are extremely triggered by confrontation, you may need to study techniques for conflict resolution. Often, speak to a psychiatrist or other specialist of behavioral well-being to learn how to handle the emotions created by these disputes.

Health issues can cause anxiety:

An upsetting or difficult health diagnosis, such as cancer or any chronic disease, can cause anxiety or even worsen it. Because of the personal and immediate emotions, it creates, this form of a trigger is very strong.

By being motivated and involved with your therapist, you will help alleviate anxiety induced by health problems. It can also be helpful to speak with a therapist, since they may help you learn to control the feelings throughout the diagnosis.

Caffeine can be a cause:

Many people depend on their cup of joy in the morning to get up, but it might potentially trigger anxiety or intensify it. Individuals with a social anxiety disorder and panic disorder are highly susceptible to the anxiety-inducing impact of caffeine, according to one report. Act by replacing non-caffeinated alternatives wherever possible to reduce caffeine consumption.

Use of medications can cause anxiety:

Symptoms of anxiety can be induced by some prescription and OTC (over-the-counter) medicines. That's because, in these drugs, active ingredients can make you feel unwell or uneasy. In the mind and body, these thoughts will set off a sequence of events that can contribute to increased signs of anxiety. Medications which may induce anxiety include:

- Medications for congestion and cough
- Pills for birth control
- Medications for weight loss

Speak to the psychiatrist regarding how you feel about these medications and search for an option that doesn't cause the anxiety or make your symptoms worse.

Skipping your meals can cause anxiety:

Your blood sugar will drop when you do not eat. This can add to shaking hands and a tummy that rumbles. Anxiety can also be triggered. For several factors, consuming healthy meals is vital. It offers energy and vital nutrients for you. Snacks that are healthy are a perfect way to avoid low blood sugar, nausea, and symptoms of agitation or nervousness if you cannot find time for 3 meals a day. Now, the mood may be influenced by food.

Financial concerns can cause anxiety:

Concerns over spending cash or getting debt will induce anxiety. Unexpected expenses or worries for finances are often the causes. Learning to handle certain kinds of triggers, such as by a financial planner, can involve finding professional help. Feeling like you have a friend in the phase and a reference will reduce your concern.

Over-thinking or pessimistic thinking can cause anxiety:

Your mind regulates more of your body, and with anxiety, that is probably real. The phrases you speak to yourself will cause greater feelings of distress when you're angry or irritated. When speaking about yourself, whether you want to use a lot of derogatory terms, it is good to try to refocus your vocabulary and emotions before you move on this road. In this approach, interacting with a psychiatrist will be extremely effective.

Social events or parties can be a cause:

You are not alone if a room full of people doesn't sound like fun. Events that cause you to speak or communicate with others you don't meet will induce nervous stimuli and may be classified as a social anxiety disorder. You should still carry along a friend where possible to help relieve the worries or pain. But engaging with a therapist to identify coping strategies that render certain incidents more stable in the long run is often important.

Stress can trigger anxiety:

Regular stressors such as traffic delays or catching your train will induce anxiety for everyone. Although, as well as many other health conditions, long-term or persistent stress may contribute to long-term distress and deteriorating symptoms. Stress may also relate to habits such as eating meals, not having enough sleep, or consuming alcohol. Such factors may induce anxiety or worsen it, too.

It also needs developing coping skills to treat and avoid stress. When they get problematic or overwhelming, a psychiatrist or psychologist will certainly help you learn to understand and manage the causes of stress.

Personal triggers can be a cause:

It can be challenging to recognize these causes, but an expert in mental wellbeing is qualified to help you recognize them. These can start with a place a smell or even a song. Personal stimuli remind you of a negative experience or painful incident in your life, either knowingly or unconsciously. People with PTSD (Post-traumatic stress disorder) also face environmental stimuli that trigger anxiety.

Performances or public events can cause anxiety:

A typical cause of anxiety is public speaking, competing in a race, communicating in front of the manager, or even simply reading aloud. A psychologist or therapist will collaborate with you and find how to feel more relaxed in these environments, whether a career or hobbies need this. Strong input from friends and family will also make you feel more relaxed and secure.

It can take time to recognize personal causes, but it's important for you to learn to resolve them.

Tips for identifying your personal triggers:

When you are able to understand and identify the causes, you will learn to prevent and deal with them. To control the stimuli as they arise, you will develop unique coping mechanisms.

For identifying stimuli, here are three popular tips:

- Start a diary. Write down anytime you feel the anxiety and note what you believe might have contributed to the cause. Any app will help you control your anxiety, too.

- Be realistic with yourself. As anxiety can trigger negative feelings and low self-evaluation. Due to the anxiety responses, this may render identifying stimuli difficult. To recognize how they can influence you now, be gentle with yourself, and able to explore stuff about the past.

- Work alongside a therapist. It may be challenging to recognize any anxiety causes, but an expert in mental wellbeing has the experience that can support you. In order to locate causes, they can use journaling, talk counseling, or other strategies.

Symptoms that can tell about anxiety:

The most common anxiety signs include:

- Uncontrollable concern
- Muscle stress
- Fear
- A rapid heartbeat
- Sleep trouble or insomnia
- Physical pain
- Difficulty in concentration
- Tingling
- Sensation on the edge
- Irritability
- Restlessness

You may have a generalized anxiety disorder (GAD) if you encounter these signs frequently for six months or longer. There are also several forms of anxiety disorders. The signs could be different for them than for GAD. With panic disorder, for example, you can experience:

- A fast heartbeat
- Tremble
- Feeling as if you are closing your throat
- Sweating
- Shaking

What you can do to cure anxiety triggers?

It's important to get treatment whether you think you're worried too hard or assume you have an anxiety condition. It is also difficult to recognize anxiety and, with time, the signs become normal. It is normal to experience occasional anxiety, but there are no persistent feelings of stress, dread, or terror. It's a warning that you should pursue clinical assistance. Through talking to your doctor, start the conversation. They can resolve the symptoms, conduct a personal history, and undertake a physical test. They may try to rule out any other physical conditions that could cause complications, too. Your doctor may want to treat you with medicine from there onwards. They can even refer you, such as a counselor or therapist, to a mental well-being specialist. A mixture of talk therapy (psychotherapy) and medicine may be used by these physicians to manage anxiety and avoid stimuli.

Occasional anxiety is normal, but it's not common to experience persistent feelings of dread, worry, or fear. It's a warning that you can seek clinical assistance. The positive thing is that fear is a behavioral well-being disorder that is easily treatable. Many individuals with anxiety don't get help, though. You should get treatment if your fear is hindering your day-to-day existence. An expert in mental wellbeing will help you with a care strategy that helps ease your symptoms and lets you deal with the causes of your anxiety.

1.3 Possible causes and common symptoms of anxiety (anxiety in a relationship)

General causes of anxiety:

Doctors do not really understand what induces conditions like anxiety. It is currently known that in individuals who are vulnerable to it, such stressful events will cause anxiety. Genetics can play a role in anxiety as well. Anxiety may be triggered by underlying health problems in certain situations which may be the earliest symptoms of a physical disease rather than a mental one. At the same time, an individual can suffer from one or even more anxiety disorders. Some mental health problems such as bipolar disorder or depression can also be followed by it. This is specifically true in generalized anxiety disorder, which most frequently follows another mental or anxiety disorder.

A mental illness, the results of drugs, any physical injury, or a mixture of these can often induce anxiety. The initial assignment of the psychiatrist is to see whether your anxiety is a result of some medical problems. These mental disorders involve important triggers of anxiety:

- Panic disorder: Beside anxiety, palpitations (feeling the heartbeat), dizziness, or shortness of breath are typical signs of panic disorders. Amphetamines an overactive thyroid, coffee, irregular heartbeats, and other heart defects (like mitral valve prolapse) can also trigger the same symptoms.
- Phobic disorders
- Generalized anxiety disorder
- Stress disorders

Anxiety may also be triggered by these popular external factors:

- Symptoms of medical illness (like hypoglycemia, heart attack, heat stroke,)
- Work burden
- Stress in a private partnership like marriage
- School Burden
- Stress from a chronic medical problem
- Financial pressure
- Stress, like a pandemic, from unexpected or unknown global events
- Stress from world affairs or political concerns
- Stress from psychological trauma, such as a loved one's death
- Side effects of Medicines
- Usage with an illegal substance or cocaine
- In conditions as common as high altitude vomiting, emphysema, or pulmonary embolism (blood clot in the lung vessels), loss of oxygen

Major symptoms of anxiety:

Although the signs of anxiety differ from person to person, the body usually responds to anxiety in a very particular manner.

Your body goes on high alert when you feel nervous, checking for possible danger and triggering your fight or flight reactions. Some typical symptoms of anxiety, as a response, include:

- Difficulty reflecting or specifically worrying about something other than the issue that you are concerned about
- Nervousness, restlessness, or being nervous
- Performing certain actions over and over again
- Fast heart rhythm
- Fast respiration or hyperventilation
- Trembling or twitching of muscles
- Sweating increased or strong
- Weak and lethargy
- Insomnia
- A deep urge to eliminate the items that cause your anxiety
- Gastrointestinal or stomach disorders, such as constipation diarrhea, or gas

- Obsessions with certain emotions, a symptom of obsessive-compulsive disorder (OCD)
- Post-traumatic stress disorder (PTSD) is distress about a real-life occurrence or incident that has happened in the past.

Panic attacks:

A panic attack is a rapid outbreak of discomfort or distress that occurs in minutes and includes at least 4 of the following signs:

- Palpitations
- Trembling or shaking
- Numbness or symptoms of tingling (paresthesia)
- Sensation of suffocation
- Sensation of suffocation
- Fear of going mad or losing hold of yourself
- Dizziness, a weak or light-headed sensation
- Difficulty in breathing or smothering
- Pains in the chest or tightness
- Gastrointestinal problems or discomfort
- Feeling hot or cold

- Feeling detached from reality or oneself, known as depersonalization and derealization
- Scared of death

In situations other than anxiety problems, there are several signs of anxiety that may arise. Normally, this is the situation of panic attacks. Panic attack signs are close to those of heart attacks, respiratory issues, problems of the thyroid, and other diseases. As a consequence, people who have panic disorder can make regular visits to doctor's offices or emergency rooms. They can feel that they encounter health problems other than anxiety that are life-threatening.

Some common symptoms of relationship anxiety:

In various forms, relationship anxiety will turn up. At some point, most individuals feel a little uncertain about their partnership, particularly in the initial stages of dating and developing a commitment. This is not uncommon, so you do not need to worry about passing on worries or concerns in general, especially if they don't bother you very much. Sometimes, though, these nervous thoughts develop and expand into your everyday life. Here is a glance at certain possible symptoms of fear in relationships:

Doubting feelings of your partner for you:

You traded I love you (or maybe I truly, truly, really like you) for yourself. They still seem pleased to see you and make nice movements, like going out of their way and seeing you home or taking your lunch. But the nagging doubt you somehow cannot shake: they do not even value you. Perhaps they are reluctant to respond to physical intimacy. Or for many hours, even a day, they don't respond to messages. You question whether their thoughts have shifted because they unexpectedly appear a little distant. Everyone feels the same way from time - to - time, but if you do have relationship anxiety, these worries may become a fixation.

The unnecessary seeking of reassurance:

In depression and social anxiety disorder, prolonged reassurance-seeking is often frequent. Some researchers say that interpersonal dependence is correlated with unnecessary reassurance-seeking. Interpersonal dependence relates to the dependence of an individual on others for continuous judgment and acceptance. Individuals who show extreme reassurance-seeking behavior may be fearful of getting or not acknowledging a poor assessment.

Having confusion if you matter to your partner or not:

The most popular term of relationship distress refers to underlying issues. Do I matter? Or are you going to be there for me? In a relationship, this speaks to a basic desire to belong, connect, and feel secure. You could worry, for instance, that:

If you were not alive, your wife might not notice you either.

Only because of what you are doing for them, they want to stay with you.

When something major comes up, they do not offer support or help.

Missing your good times:

Really not sure why you're coping with anxiety in relationships? Take a step back and question yourself: Are you wasting more time stressing than loving this relationship? This may be the case during hard periods. Yet you are still dealing with any intimacy anxiety if you sound this way more frequently than not.

Showing yourself in silence:

Another symptom associated with many mental health disorders is self-silencing. One study said that in order to appease their mate, women who are vulnerable to rejection would be inclined to participate in self-silencing. People who are self-silent cannot communicate with their partner their beliefs, tastes, or emotions, especially when such thoughts are not similar to their partner's. In an effort to avoid rejection, individuals seem to indulge in self-silencing actions to look close to those whose recognition they seek. Over time, to maintain the relationship, an individual can silence oneself and make sacrifices. This, though, has the ability to lower satisfaction in relationships.

Fear of break up:

A relationship that is good will make you feel loved, secure, and happy. It's completely natural to want to hang on to these emotions and expect that nothing can break the bond. But often these feelings can transform into a constant fear of your wife leaving you. When you change your actions in order to gain their continued love, this anxiety will become problematic. For instance, you might:

Stop presenting problems that are essential to you in your relationship, such as constant lateness,

You think a lot about them being angry at you, even though they don't appear to be angry at you.

Avoid doing stuff that annoys them, such as wearing your shoes inside the home, while your wife does

Providing accommodation to your partner:

Partner accommodation is the other party's reaction to an anxious person. This is a typical result found in couples where obsessive-compulsive personality disorder is prevalent in one or more persons.

Vandalizing the relationship:

In relationship anxiety, sabotaging or vandalizing activities can

have roots. Examples of items that a relationship could sabotage include:

Choosing arguments for the mate

Checking partnership thresholds, like taking lunch with an ex without asking your wife

Drive them out by insisting that while you are in trouble, nothing is wrong.

You do not consciously do this stuff, but the underlying purpose, whether you know it or not, is typically to decide how much your spouse cares. For example, you might assume that refusing your attempts to drive them away shows that they still value you. Although, this implicit motivation is very complicated for the wife to pick up on.

Having doubt for long-term compatibility factor:

Relationship anxiety may make you wonder whether, particularly when things are going well in the relationship, you and your spouse are really happy. You might even be telling yourself if you are really content, or if you really believe you are. In reaction, you may start concentrating your mind on small distinctions, enjoying punk music, but you are more of a folk-rock guy, and overemphasizing their significance.

Reading into their actions and words:

A desire to overthink the language and action of your companion can often indicate discomfort in relationships. They do not like holding hands. Or, they focus on holding all their current furniture as you take the plunge to move in together. Sure, both of these may be indicators of possible concern. Yet they are more prone to have sweaty palms or really always enjoy the set of living rooms.

What actually causes relationship anxiety?

It will take patience and committed self-exploration to determine what's causing your anxiety because there is not a single straightforward cause. You may also have a rough time with your own finding possible triggers. You might not be sure of a trigger for the anxiety, but regardless of how it occurs, the underlying causes typically reflect a need for connection. There are some prevalent variables that may play a role:

The capability of asking the question:

A questioning nature may also play into anxiety in relationships. Before agreeing on a path, you can need to question yourself about the potential outcome of a scenario. Or maybe you just have a pattern of considering any choice carefully. Even after you have made them, if you choose to ask a lot of questions regarding your actions, you will actually spend some time challenging your relationship, too. It's not really a concern here. In reality, it is typically safe to take time to reflect on your decisions, particularly essential ones. If you find yourself trapped in an endless loop of confusion and self-doubt that does not go somewhere positive, it might become a challenge, however.

Past experiences of relationship:

You will continue to be influenced by reminders of incidents that occurred in the past, even though you believe you have really gotten over them. As a past partner, you may be more prone to encounter relationship anxiety:

- Misled you on the essence of your relationship
- Lied regarding the emotions they have towards you
- Cheated on you
- Dumped you out of the blue

When you have been hurt, it's not rare to have trouble putting trust in anyone again, particularly if the new relationship displays no indicators of dishonesty or manipulation. Any stimuli will always remind you of the past, if you are conscious of them or not, and evoke fear and uncertainty.

Your experience of attachment style:

As an adult, the attachment style you establish in childhood may have a huge effect on our relationships. You would possibly establish a stable attachment style if your parent reacted immediately to your requirements and provided support and love. Your relationship style might be less stable if they did not fulfill your expectations regularly or let you grow individually. Insecure attachment patterns may lead in different ways to relationship anxiety:

On the other side, the nervous attachment will often contribute to worries of your companion abandoning you suddenly.

Avoidant commitment can contribute to anxiety about the degree of devotion you make or intensify intimacy.

Bear in mind that getting an unstable relational style does not mean that you are likely to experience anxiety in relationships at all times. You cannot totally alter your attachment style much like you cannot change from one kind of attitude to another, but you can definitely make enough adjustments where an unstable attachment style does not keep you down in existence.

Low self-esteem:

Poor self-esteem may also lead to anxiety and insecurity in relationships. Any older research indicates that when witnessing self-doubt, persons with low self-esteem are more prone to suspect the emotions of their mate. As a form of projection, this may happen. In other terms, it would be better for you to accept that your girlfriend thinks the same way towards you through getting disappointed in you. On the other side, individuals with greater self-esteem appeared to assert themselves by their relationship when self-doubt is experienced.

Can you cure it?

It may not seem like it at the moment, but it might be necessary to conquer relationship anxiety, but it requires considerable time and commitment. And doing so usually requires more than just being informed that your relationship is all right. Anxiety may not always indicate that the relationship has an underlying issue, and they may still be well-loved, but once they have had a sense that something is good, that they are genuinely healthy and protected, the anxiety is likely to continue.

In order to better treat and control relationship anxiety, some researchers recommend couple counseling, such as couples based psycho-educational courses. The efficacy of a single psycho-educational session was tested by researchers in a report. The aim of the session was to discuss the behavioral trends correlated with partner accommodation, relationship anxiety, including self-silencing, and constantly looking for reassurance. The researchers have observed that couples with relationship anxiety have a reduced rate of reassurance seeking and self-silencing after one session. For the spouse with anxiety, the non-anxious companion has shown reduced levels of accommodation. Various kinds of treatment for partners include:

l Psychotherapy psychodynamics

l Cognitive existential couples therapy

l Cognitive-behavioral conjoint therapy

l Behavioral couples therapy

Since the relationship anxiety has common symptoms with other anxiety conditions, certain clinicians can consider communicating with the anxiety spouse only. Others can prescribe useful anxiety disorder therapies, including cognitive-behavioral therapy (CBT), acceptance and motivation counseling, and mindfulness. Following individual CBT, there is a diverse variety of consequences. This range of responses can be consistent with the degree of hostility and critique experienced before care during some couple encounters. Doctors should always recommend that the non-anxious companion be included in the recovery plan. The partner's position is usually a co-therapist. Some persons may need treatment. Anxiety drugs include selective inhibitors of serotonin reuptake and selective inhibitors of noradrenaline reuptake. For the management of relationship anxiety, doctors may not yet provide guidelines. To properly understand and handle it, more studies into this form of anxiety are necessary.

1.4 Natural remedies for chronic anxiety you never heard about

Some anxiety is a natural part of life. It's a side effect of working in a culture that is always unpredictable. However, anxiety is not always bad. This makes you mindful of the danger, prompts you to be coordinated and alert, and enables you to assess risks. Even, there is best to act before it snowballs as anxiety becomes a constant challenge. Your standard of living can be profoundly influenced by uncontrolled anxiety. Take charge by trying the below ideas out.

Having chamomile tea:

In order to calm hurt feelings and encourage sleep, a chamomile teacup is a popular home remedy. Strong support against generalized anxiety disorder can also be Chamomile. The study showed that people taking capsules of German chamomile (220 mg up-to 5 times a day) had a higher reduction in test scores that measure symptoms of anxiety than those who used placebo

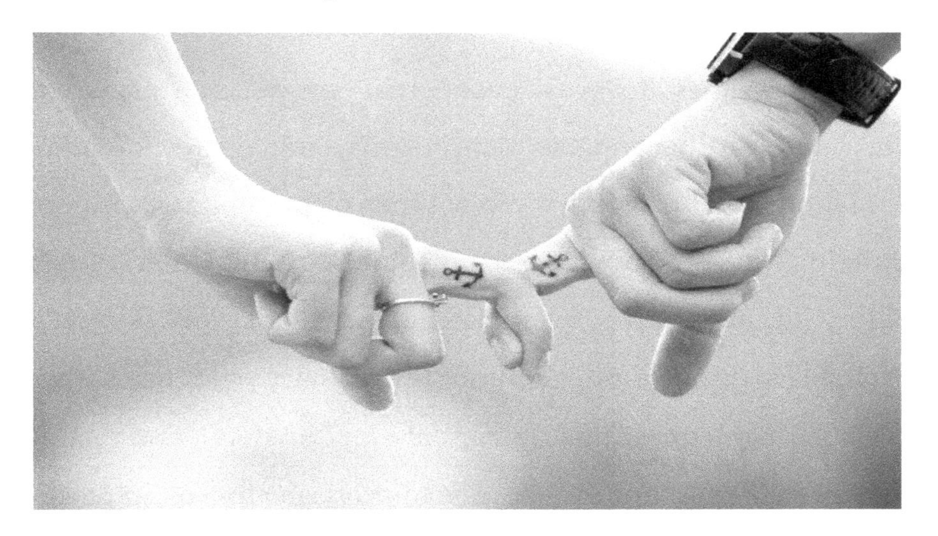

Use of Herbal teas:

Many herbal teas aim to relieve sleep and assist with anxiety. Some individuals find the tea producing and drinking phase calming, although some teas can have a more direct impact on the brain, resulting in decreased anxiety. Study findings indicate that chamomile can change levels of a stress hormone, cortisol.

Stay fast and active:

For both your physical and mental well-being, daily exercise is healthy. Daily activity helps with certain individuals, as well as medicine to relieve anxiety. And it is not a short-term fix; after

working out for hours, you will feel anxiety relief.

Use of cannabidiol oil:

CBD oil comes from a plant that grows marijuana. A derivative of the cannabis plant, or marijuana, is cannabidiol (CBD) oil. CBD oil, unlike other types of marijuana, does not contain THC or tetrahydrocannabinol, a drug that causes highs. In alternative healthcare stores, CBD oil is easily available without a prescription. Preliminary evidence shows that it has substantial potential for anxiety and panic reduction. Physicians will be able to prescribe this oil in places where legal marijuana is lawful.

To get rid of smoking:

During difficult times, smokers often search for a cigarette. Yet, like alcohol drinking, when you are stressed, taking a puff on a cigarette is a fast remedy that may intensify anxiety over time. It has been stated that the sooner you start cigarette smoking in life, the greater the likelihood that you will later develop an anxiety disorder. Research also indicates that nicotine and other ingredients in cigarette smoke alter anxiety-related pathways in the brain.

Manage your time:

If they have too many obligations at once, some people feel

anxious. These can include activities related to family, work, and health. Getting a strategy in place for the next step that is required will help to keep this anxiety aside. Efficient techniques for time management may help individuals concentrate on one task at a time. As well as avoiding the temptation to multitask, online calendars and book based planners will help. Some people find that it will allow them to achieve certain tasks with less stress by breaking down big projects into manageable steps.

Don't take excessive alcohol:

Alcohol is a regular sedative. When your nerves are damaged, a finger of whisky or drinking a glass of wine can at first relax you. However, after the sensation is gone, anxiety can come roaring back. If you focus on alcohol instead of addressing the source of the issue to reduce anxiety, you can develop alcohol dependency.

Ditch your caffeine dose:

Caffeine is not your buddy if you have persistent anxiety. Caffeine can trigger nervousness and anxiety, none of which, if you're stressed, is pleasant. Research has shown that caffeine can cause anxiety disorders or intensify them. In individuals with panic disorder, it can often trigger panic attacks. Eliminating caffeine in certain individuals may develop

symptoms of anxiety largely.

Use of Herbal supplements:

Many herbal supplements appear to relieve anxiety, much like herbal teas. However, these arguments are supported by limited statistical proof. Working with a specialist who is informed about herbal remedies and their possible interactions with other medications is important.

Use of Herbal supplements:

Many herbal supplements tend to relieve anxiety, much like herbal teas. However, these arguments are supported by limited scientific proof. Working with a specialist who is informed about herbal remedies and their possible interactions with the other medicines is important.

The practice of relaxation exercises:

In reaction to anxiety, certain individuals instinctively relax their muscles and clench their jaws. Progressive exercise for relaxing can help. Try to lay in a relaxed posture then, starting with the toes then moving up to your shoulders and chin, steadily constrict and relax each muscle group.

Meditate yourself:

A primary purpose of meditation is to eliminate chaotic emotions from the mind and substitute them with the current moment's sense of peace and mindfulness. Meditation is popular for tension and anxiety reduction. It has been reported that certain anxiety effects can be reduced by 30 minutes of regular meditation and function as an antidepressant.

Spending some time with your animals:

Companionship, love, and comfort are provided by pets. For those with a range of mental health challenges, including anxiety, pets may be helpful. Although certain individuals enjoy dogs, cats, and other small animals, persons with allergies would be happy to hear that to offer help, the pet must be fluffy. Research showed that in older adults, caring for crickets might enhance psychological well-being. Spending time around animals will also decrease trauma-related anxiety and tension. Any of these symptoms may also be solved by brushing and time spent with horses.

Get some healthy sleep:

A common sign of anxiety is insomnia. Making sleep a matter of importance by:

- Only sleep at night while you are tired.
- Not in bed with your cell, mobile, or machine
- Not watching reading TV in bed
- Go to sleep every night at the same time
- If you cannot sleep, do not toss and turn in your bed; get up and walk into another room before you feel tired.
- Keeping your place calm and dim
- Caffeine, big meals, and cigarettes are stopped until going to bed
- Writing down your thoughts before heading to bed

Eating a healthy reasonable diet:

In certain individuals, obesity, low blood sugar levels, or additives in packaged foods, such as artificial flavorings, artificial colors, and preservatives, may induce mood changes. A high-sugar diet can also have an effect on temperament.

Review your dietary patterns if your anxiety deepens after dining. Keep hydrated, consume a nutritious diet high in vegetable complex carbohydrates, and lean proteins, and fruits, and minimize refined foods.

Writing habit:

It may become more comfortable when having a way to communicate anxiety. Any research indicates that journaling as well as other ways of writing may allow individuals to interact with anxiety better. For instance, another research showed that creative writing can help children and adolescents overcome anxiety.

To try out aromatherapy:

To encourage wellness and well-being, aromatherapy incorporates fragrant essential oils. It is necessary to inhale the oils directly or apply them to a diffuser or warm bath. Aromatherapy has been seen in studies:

- Helps to calm you
- Mood improves
- Helps in sleeping
- Reduces heart rate and hypertension
- The following are few natural oils used to alleviate anxiety:

- Ylang Ylang
- Bergamot
- Sage Clary
- Lavender
- Grapefruit

Shallow, rapid breathing with anxiety is prevalent. It may lead to a panic attack, high heart rate, or even light-headedness or dizziness. Deep breathing exercises will help maintain regular breathing habits and minimize discomfort, the systematic

practice of taking long, steady, deep breaths.

Some other treatments:

The anxiety that is recurrent or interferes with the capacity of an individual to work needs care. Therapy is the most common type of treatment where there is no underlying physical health disorder, such as thyroid problems. Therapy may encourage a person to realize what induces their anxiety. It will also help to bring significant improvements in lifestyles and to function through stress. Cognitive-behavioral therapy (CBT) is considered one of the most successful anxiety treatments. The aim is to make an individual recognize how their feelings and behavior are influenced by their perceptions and to substitute certain responses with optimistic or productive alternatives. CBT may assist with generalized anxiety and anxiety linked to a particular condition such as work or trauma. Medications can also help control persistent anxiety in an individual. Drugs in any of the following classes can be recommended by a doctor:

Benzodiazepines, such as Xanax, and Valium, are anti-anxiety medications.

Medicines for sleeping while anxiety starts to interfere with sleep.

Antidepressants, like Prozac, are called selective serotonin

reuptake blockers or inhibitors.

Natural remedies for anxiety may substitute conventional medications or complement them.

Chapter 02: Recognizing your major Anxiety-triggers with their solutions

In this chapter, all the basic methods of recognizing your major anxiety-triggers with their solutions are given in detail. How to acknowledge the fear of collapse and being vulnerable or abandonment and how to cope up with these, how to understand the signs or symptoms of fear of failure and not being important and how to overcome this; these aspects are discussed in depth and detail. How to know and control your fear of past experience and fear of entering into intimacy are also mentioned in this chapter.

2.1 Fear of collapse and being vulnerable or abandonment

Fear of collapse in anxiety:

Anxiety is a disorder whose side effects will potentially contribute to the physical breakdown in the long term.

Although the feeling like you are about to collapse or drop out may be triggered by extreme anxiety disorders, it is generally very unlikely when someone does: it is far more common than you have long-term, chronic anxiety that does not diminish (which usually causes problems such as psychosis, but may often be a product of a rather difficult lifestyle and a loss of strategies for coping). We are going to learn about the signs and side effects of distress that can contribute to long-term breakdown, as well as learn about certain coping strategies that help you alleviate the fear until it triggers physical collapse.

Anxiety signs and symptoms of collapse:

Anxiety produces fainting very, very rarely. It can, because anxiety triggers muscle weakness and hyperventilation, and how you respond to it (such as holding your breath) will lead you to collapse in certain instances. What anxiety does is cause a range of signals that stress the body and making it feel like giving up. Those signs include:

Rapid heartbeat rate:

Your heart rate may speeds up as you feel upset. A raised heart rate may cause you to believe which you are going to collapse from a heart attack, in association with pain in the chest from fast breathing and stress in the muscles. In addition, adrenaline in the body is emitted by a rapid pulse, the effects of which may trigger symptoms of exhaustion and fatigue. Tension Headache / Stomach. These effects are signs that your anxiety is now controlling your body. Worrying can allow the production of stomach acids to rise, which can contribute to ulcers and/or stomach aches. When the internal discomfort becomes tangible, the emotional pressure of constant negative thinking loops that feel inescapable also has the impact of having the head hurt.

Sweating is your body:

Sweating is very associated with anxiety and may often likely contribute to collapsing issue. Sweat allows the body to lose fluids which may induce exhaustion, allowing the body to experience a great deal of discomfort. The 60% of the water that makes you up maintains all of your cells working well, reproducing nutrients, and maintaining the body. This is partially why the body without food can go longer than it does without water. The symptoms may involve dizziness and fatigue while your body is slightly dehydrated. It is understood that extreme dehydration leads to fainting. For this cause, for individuals who encounter anxiety, hydration is very necessary.

Hyperventilation:

Anxiety will also lead you to breathe very fast, which extracts carbon dioxide from your body, what it requires to flourish. This induces constriction of the blood arteries that flow through the brain which prevents the nervous system from getting the blood it needs. Although anxiety symptoms might not last long enough to contribute to fainting (that is possible), hyperventilation is more likely to actually trigger dizziness, chest pain, and a sensation of numbness in your body that mimics the sensation that you are going to pass out.

Shaking feeling:

A significant part of your muscles contracts involuntarily as your body shivers or shakes. This is because, if they have to, they are training themselves to move fast. With all the muscles, the nervous system checks in and makes sure they're ready for combat. However, both psychologically and physically, the pressure on the muscle, and the spontaneous aspect of the movement is exhausting. None of these signs tend to contribute specifically to collapse or fainting, as you can tell. But they do build an experience that may sound like the need to collapse often. In an anxiety attack, you can also sit down or feel so scared and helpless that you know you have to lie down instantly. But they do not seem to contribute to the actual passing out that most people anticipate as they think about collapse.

Keeping anxiety under your control:

You simply have to hold the anxiety in control in order to stop this sensation of collapse. There are several various strategies to prevent your anxiety attacks from exhausting you to a point of collapse, safely, naturally, and inexpensively. Examples of each of these include:

Practicing Yoga or Meditation:

Rituals and exercises intended to calm your mind and body will help you step beyond yourself and let go of the discomfort that triggers all of the symptoms. By offering you a mental break and physical, as well as a more optimistic perspective on life, doing this one time a day will significantly decrease the overall tension. They will also help you in improving your breathing, which is necessary for keeping away collapse.

Get proper sleep:

Feeling anxious may make it difficult to sleep, yet all the indicators of anxiety will make it very necessary for the body to have an opportunity to refresh and rebuild all the cells that hold you going. A known source of physical failure is often sleeplessness, so just try to sleep whatever it will take. Try to develop routines that involve a fixed bedtime, shutting off all lights, and even reading something to yourself for example from a relaxing book of stimulating images or rhymes, such as one that you loved listening to or reading as a kid.

Keep a Journal or Diary:

Writing your ideas and emotions down will help you spot the ideas that do not make sense or others that move in a circle and encourage you to work beyond them, finding out why you think them and what would be more positive or constructive to think. Without the burden of other people criticizing you for it, it is often an incentive to express what you truly think, which can be quite soothing or calming the freedom to have.

Have Group counseling:

It will be good to know that in your emotions you are not isolated, this will help dissuade you from the belief that you deserve dissatisfaction or that you should live with it, it would be obvious to you that other individuals with symptoms similar to yours deserve satisfaction and need assistance, and will then persuade you that you do too.

It also has much to do with your mindset not falling into pieces from anxiety than your physical signs, since your attitude is what decides if the symptoms persist over the amount of time it needs to contribute to failure. Although you can feel like collapsing during an assault, think of it as the body warning you of what may happen in the long run if you don't take action to fix the issue.

Fear of being vulnerable or abandonment in anxiety:

The overwhelming anxiety that those close to you would quit is the fear of abandonment. Everyone can have a fear of abandonment. It may be profoundly embedded in a painful event you experienced in adulthood, as a kid or a disturbing relationship. It will be nearly difficult to sustain healthy relationships if you fear abandonment. In order to stop being hurt, this paralyzing fear will cause you to wall off yourself. Or you may be damaging relationships unintentionally. Acknowledging that you feel this way is the first move toward conquering your anxiety. On your own or through counseling, you will be willing to resolve your concerns. Yet apprehension of abandonment can also be part of a treatment-needing personality disorder.

Various forms of fear of abandonment:

You will be scared that somebody you respect would literally leave and not return. You will worry that your emotional needs may be neglected by others. In a relationship with a friend, parent, or partner, anyone will hold you back.

Emotional abandonment fear:

It can be less obvious than being physically abandoned, but it is no less painful. Everyone has emotional needs. You could feel unloved, unappreciated, and isolated when those needs are not fulfilled. And when you are in a friendship with someone who's physically there, you might feel really lonely. If particularly as a child, you have undergone emotional neglect of the past, you will live in constant fear that it may happen again.

Abandonment anxiety in your relationships:

In a relationship, you might be terrified of making yourself be insecure. You can have trust problems and stress about your relationship excessively. It may make your spouse suspicious of you. Your anxieties may trigger the other individual to pull back in time, perpetuating the loop.

Abandonment fear in children:

For babies and toddlers, going through a separation anxiety period is completely normal. When a parent or caregiver needs to quit, they can scream, cry, or decline to let go. At this point, children have a difficult time knowing when or whether the individual would return or not. They outgrow their anxiety when they continue to realize the loved ones are back. With most adolescents, this occurs during their third birthday.

Symptoms and signs of fear of abandonment:

You may know any of these symptoms and indications if you fear abandonment:

- Overly sensitive of critique
- Difficulty having acquaintances unless you can be certain you want them
- Difficulty finding trust in someone
- Take drastic action to avoid resistance or breakup
- Being so easily attached to others, and almost as easily moving on
- Unhealthy relationship history
- Difficulty sticking to a relationship
- Self- blaming when it doesn't work out
- Working too much for the other person to please
- Staying in such a relationship that you think is unhealthy

Reasons of fear of abandonment:

Some big factors are below:

Abandonment issues in your relationships:

In your present relationship, whether you fear abandonment, it could be related to having been rejected emotionally or physically in the past. For instance:

- You may have witnessed a parent or caregiver's death or desertion as a child.
- You may have witnessed parental neglect.
- You have gone through a loved one's prolonged sickness.
- Your colleagues or peers could have rejected you.
- A loving partner may have unexpectedly abandoned you or acted in an untrustworthy way.

These activities will give rise to abandonment fear.

Borderline personality disorder:

Another personality condition in which extreme fear of abandonment may play a part is a borderline personality disorder. Other indications and signs can include:

- Difficulty in being isolated or alone
- Unstable experiences in relationship
- Extreme impulsivity
- Self-image distorted
- Mood swings and inappropriate frustration

Some persons with borderline personality disorder claim they have been physically or sexually abused as children. Others ended up in constant conflict or had members of their families with the same illness.

Avoidant personality disorder:

Personality disorder which involves abandonment fear resulting in the feeling of person socially inadequate or inhibited is called avoidant personality disorder.

Some indications and signs are:

- Nervousness
- Avoidance of self-imposed social isolation and group activities

- Intense anxiety of being judged or rejected negatively
- Poor self-esteem
- In social situations, discomfort

Separation anxiety disorder:

They might have a separation anxiety disorder if a child cannot outgrow separation anxiety and this interferes with everyday activities. Some symptoms and indicators of separation anxiety disorder may include:

- When apart from loved ones, physical problems, including stomachache or headache,
- Attacks of anger
- Refusal to leave home or be left home lonely without a loved one
- Distress at the idea of being detached from loved ones
- Nightmares that include separation from loved ones
- Teens and adults can also suffer from a separation anxiety disorder.

Chronic effects of fear of abandonment:

Long-term consequences of abandonment fear may include:

- Difficult interactions between friends and intimate partners
- Issues of Trust
- Low esteem for oneself
- Issues of Anger
- Codependence
- Mood swings
- Fear of being intimate
- Depression
- Anxiety disorders
- Panic disorder

Examples of fear of vulnerability or abandonment:

Here are some illustrations of what it may be like to fear abandonment:

Your insecurity is so powerful that you do not encourage yourself to get attached to someone sufficiently to let it happen.

Obsessively, you worry about the supposed flaws and what people can think about you.

No abandonment, no attachment, you would imagine.

You are the greatest pleaser for strangers. You don't want to take any risks if you are going to appreciate anyone enough to hang around.

When you feel slighted, you overreact.

When anyone gives a touch of critique or gets angry at you in some way, you are totally devastated.

You feel deficient and unappealing.

And when the other individual is asking for freedom, you are clingy.

You abandon your romantic partner so that they cannot break up with you.

You are always suspicious, jealous, or critical of your mate.

Fear of abandonment is not a mental health condition that is diagnosable, although it may surely be recognized and treated. Fear of abandonment may also be part of diagnosable personality disorder or some other treatable illness.

How to heal abandonment issues?

There are several steps you should do to start healing once you understand the fear of abandonment. Cut some slack on yourself to avoid the severe self-judgment. Remind yourself all of the positive characteristics that make you a strong partner and friend. Speak regarding the fear of abandonment

& how it happened, to the other individual. But be careful of what you are expecting from others. Explain where you're coming from, just don't make anything for them to fix the fear of abandonment. Don't demand more than is fair of them. Work to preserve friendships and to develop your network of support. Your self-worth and sense of identity may be improved by good friendships. Consider going to a trained psychiatrist if you find something unmanageable. Person therapy can help you.

Helping someone with abandonment issues:

If anybody you meet is struggling with fear of abandonment, here are a few methods to try:

- Let the talk started. Encourage them, just do not encourage them to speak about it.
- In order to help, ask what you should do.
- Assure them you're not going to leave them.
- Understand the anxiety is genuine for them, whether it makes any sense to you or not.
- Suggest counseling, just do not push it. Give your help in seeking a competent psychiatrist whenever they show a need to move forward.

Seeing a doctor:

See a psychiatric professional if you've attempted but cannot cope with the fear of abandonment by your own-self, or if you have signs of nervous illness, depression, or panic disorder. For a thorough checkup, you should begin with your healthcare provider. In order to diagnose and manage the illness, they may then refer you to any mental health specialist. Personality disorders may contribute to stress, social isolation, and drug usage, without treatment.

Your relationships may be adversely impacted by the fear of abandonment. But in order to alleviate such worries, there is stuff you should try. It may be effectively handled with medication and psychotherapy while fear of abandonment is a part of larger personality disorder.

2.2 Fear of failure and not feeling important

Nobody likes failing. Fear of failure may be so high that the desire to succeed is completely overshadowed by preventing failure. Insecurity over getting something wrong leads certain persons to compromise their chances of performance unconsciously. Fear is part of the nature of humans. Together, we can discuss how, instead of having it run your life, you may use the loss to your benefit.

Understanding fear of failure:

Fear allows you to escape circumstances that are potentially harmful. Fear of failure prevents you from attempting, creates progress installs, questions regarding yourself, and may cause you to go beyond your morality. Here are the principal reasons why there is a fear of failure:

- False self-confidence: True-confident people realize that they will not necessarily succeed. Risks are prevented by an individual with weak self-confidence. They would rather play it comfortably than do a different game.
- Childhood patterns: Hyper-critical parents allow harmful mindsets to be internalized by children. They set down ultimatums and guidelines focused on fear. This makes kids feel the persistent urge to check for consent and reassurance. They take this desire into adulthood for affirmation.
- Over-personalization: We may over-identify with mistakes because of the ego. It's complicated to look at stuff like the efficiency of the effort, development potential, or extenuating conditions beyond failure.
- Perfectionism: The source of the fear of failure is also perfectionism. Failure is so dreadful and embarrassing

for perfectionists that they do not try. It becomes frightening to move out of your comfort zone.

How the Fear of Failure resists you from getting success?

You could be harmed by fear of failure in the following ways:

Losing your creativity:

Their peace of mind and the futures of others who work with

them are ruined by over-achievers. People who are so close to goodness and virtue become bigots who are self-righteous. Those whose principles become unbalanced in constructing intimate relationships slip into suffocating their family and friends with endless displays of affection and requests in exchange for support. Everyone loves succeeding. When the fear of failing is dominant, the dilemma arises. When the inevitable outcome of making errors can no longer be acknowledged, or the value of trial and error in seeking the right and most innovative approach can no longer be understood. The more you are creative, the more mistakes you are likely to make. Get used to this. Deciding to prevent mistakes will ruin the creativity, too.

More than you thought, balance matters. The sweetest dish must be balanced with some tartness. Also in the most loving human, a little egoism is valuable. And to preserve everybody's viewpoint on progress, a little disappointment is necessary. We learn about being optimistic a lot. Perhaps we will need to understand that the negative elements of our lives and interactions play an increasingly essential role in achieving progress, both at work and in life.

Organization culture that is unhealthy:

There are cultures of perfection in so many organizations

today: a collection of organizational values that any mistake is intolerable. Only clean, untainted results can do it. In an institution like that, picture the tension and fear. The persistent secrecy of the slightest blemishes. The furious finger-pointing as someone attempts to transfer the blame to everyone else for the unavoidable cock-ups and messes. As people climb big, the fast turnover, then drop suddenly from grace. The cheating, lying, data falsification, and covering topics until they become problems that are no longer hidden.

High achievers suddenly become losers:

There is an opposite of every skill that turns it into a handicap sometimes. Successful persons like to win and reach high goals. This will cause them so afraid of defeat that their lives are destroyed. If a positive attribute gets so powerful in someone's life, like success, that is on the road to being a big handicap. Achievement for several successful persons is a powerful value. On it, they have based their lives. Through whatever they do, they accomplish anything: work, school, college, arts, hobbies, sports. Every new accomplishment contributes to the strength of the meaning of their lives. Failure becomes unimaginable gradually. Maybe they have never been disappointed with something they have achieved yet because they have no practice in growing above it. Failure becomes the ultimate

nightmare: at all cost, a horrific tragedy they must escape.

The best way to achieve this is to never take a chance, stick to everything you feel you should do rigidly, work the longest hours, verify all double and triple, and be the most conservative and conscientious guy in the world. If the risk of defeat is not fenced off by relentless hard work, brutal daily hours, dedication, and harrying superiors, utilizing all other possible methods to hold it hidden. Falsify figures, cover failures, conceal something bad, ignore criticism from consumers, and continuously pass the responsibility for mistakes to someone too poor to battle back.

Missing out some reasonable opportunities:

If, because of the lure of any early achievement, any individuals struggle to find a full conclusion, even more struggle because of their loyalty driven by ego to what served in the past. With professional people, especially many who made their identities by making a crucial change years ago, you always see this. They shy away from more creativity, fearful that they could fail this time, fading the luster they are striving to maintain from the previous triumph around their titles. Besides, they claim, the achievement of anything new might also show that, after all, those successes they produced in the past were not so fantastic. In the glories of their accomplishments and egos, some persons are so heavily invested that they tend to set back opportunities for potential glory rather than face even the risk of failure.

Overcoming your fear of failure:

Figure out what is the cause of fear:

Tell yourself what could be the underlying cause of your pessimistic attitude. If you glance at the four major factors of fear of failure, what ones do you have in mind? Write about where you believe the anxiety stems from and strive as an outsider to comprehend it.

If it helps, assume that one of your closest buddies needs help. Maybe the distress derives from anything that occurred in the youth or a deep-seated fear. Naming the root of fear takes some of the intensity away.

Learn to think optimistically:

You accept what you say about yourself in several situations. Your intense argument determines how you behave and react. Our culture is concerned with achievement, but it's necessary to remember that failure is encountered by even the most accomplished individuals.

Walt Disney was dismissed from a newspaper once when they believed he was lacking in talent. He went on to establish a failing cartoon studio. He never decided to give up, and Disney

has become a household icon today.

Steve Jobs once was fired from Apple once before returning for several years as the face of the company. They would not have done that if Jobs and Disney believed in the negative review.

It's up to you to note and understand the origins of your negative self-talk. Replace pessimistic feelings for facts about you and the circumstance that are constructive. When you sense negativity coming in, you may be able to build a fresh internal script that you will aim for. The voice within your mind has a major influence on what you are doing.

Re-frame your beliefs about your goals:

Having an almost all or nothing attitude often leaves you with nothing. Get a strong vision about what you intend to achieve, but have the goal of discovering something different. You are much less prone to struggle if you still look for progress and growth. In reality, individuals are expected to fail fast and fail early. Innovation and experimentation are promoted so that they can remain on the edge. The mentality includes loss, but all the major obstacles are only resources to develop as long as they accomplish their goal of telling amazing stories.

Consider all of the potential outcomes:

It is terrifying to be uncertain of what will happen next. Taking

time to imagine the decision's future consequences. Consider the situations that are optimal and worst-case. If you have always had an ability to emotionally brace for what could happen, you'll feel stronger. Fear of the unexpected might deter you from taking on a new career. In making such a choice that is life-changing, consider the pros and cons and visualize future achievements and defeats. It could help you to get unstuck by understanding how things could work out.

Seek to learn from all the happenings:

Things might not go the way you expected, but that doesn't imply that you have failed immediately. From, whatever happens, learn. Also, a circumstance that is less than optimal can be a wonderful opportunity to make improvements and evolve. You win sometimes, you learn sometimes. Tell yourself what you have been learning. From this, how do you grow? Is there been something good emerging from such a situation? Look long enough, and the bright lining is expected to reach you. You overcome the fear of defeat because you've realized that defeat is a chance for progress rather than a death sentence.

Have your healthy backup plan:

Getting a backup strategy never hurts. The very last thing you need to do after the incident actually happened is to look for a remedy. Strong advice is this traditional adage that is hope for the best, brace for the worst.

Getting a backup strategy allows you more confidence in going on and taking measured chances. Maybe you have applied for a loan to finance a project at work. Under the worst-case situation, are there any ways you can receive the funds if you don't get the grant? Typically, there are many options to solve a crisis, but getting a backup is a perfect way to alleviate uncertainty over the future loss.

Explanation of fear of failure:

Everyone hates loss, but loss poses such a major psychological challenge to certain individuals that their desire to prevent failure exceeds their incentive to succeed. This fear of disappointment leads them, in a number of ways, to unintentionally compromise their chances of achievement. Failure can evoke emotions that, while negative, are typically not sufficient to cause a full-blown fear of failures, such as disappointment, regret, anger, frustration, confusion, and sadness. Indeed, because it is not a failure that underlies the behavior of people who have it, the term is something of a misnomer. Instead, a fear of disappointment is a fear of guilt in nature. People who are afraid of failure are motivated not to avoid failure because they cannot handle the fundamental feelings of disappointment, anger, and frustration that involve such experiences, but because failure makes them feel shame deeply as well.

Shame is a socially toxic emotion, so shame helps us feel worse for who we are rather than feeling bad for our actions (that is guilt) or our accomplishments (regret). Shame goes to the center of our egos, our beliefs, our personal well-being thoughts, and our self-esteem. Especially for those that are fearful of disappointment, the negative nature of shame makes it essential to escape the psychological challenges connected with loss by seeking subtle ways to minimize the effects of a potential failure, such as purchasing needless new clothing for a work interview rather than reading up on the business, encouraging them to use the justification that one just did not have time to prepare fully.

Some major signs and symptoms you might have a fear of failure:

The following are not standard diagnostics, however, if you find like these parameters are very typical of you, becoming a significant identifying feature since we all find these items to some degree, you might want to further explore the issue, either by reading further about it or consulting to a professional mental health counselor.

- You also get headaches, stomach aches, or other physical effects at the last minute that prohibit you from finishing the preparation.
- Failing lets you stress over what you think about other individuals.
- Failure makes you fear that you are going to lose confidence in people.
- Failing lets you wonder about the opportunity to achieve the career that you seek.

- Failing leads you to think over how capable or smart you are.
- You appear to procrastinate and run out of time to properly finish the preparations.
- In order to reduce their hopes, you try to inform others in advance that you do not expect success.
- Failure allows you to stress over disappointing individuals whose opinions you respect.
- You have difficulty imagining what you should have achieved differently to succeed until you struggle at anything.
- Tasks that prohibit you from finishing your planning, which, in reflection, were not as important as they appeared at the time, always confuse you.

What you can do when you have a failure fear?

The biggest difficulty in discussing the fear of failure is that it continues to work on an unconscious level. For starters, since you agreed to send those off by the end of the week, even though you are already about to take your final exams, you may feel it's important to finish writing out the Christmas cards. But you should do two significant things to resolve the maladaptive ways in which fear of failure will affect your behavior:

You should own your anxiety: acknowledging that failure makes you experience both terror and guilt is crucial, and having trusted people with whom you can speak about these feelings. Via unconscious attempts to undermine yourself, bringing these emotions to the surface will help keep you from voicing them, and receiving reassurance and support from trustworthy people will reinforce your feelings of self-worth while reducing the chance of failing them.

You should work on certain things that are under your control: define and focus on things of the task of planning that are under your hands. Brainstorm how to re-frame elements of the assignment that seem to be out of your control so that you recover control of them. For example, if you have struggled to find jobs because you really do not know the right people, set the aim of increasing your network by looking through your Facebook and address book and social networking connections, then reaching out to everybody you know that could help: they could know somebody who may help, even though they are not in your sector.

2.3 Fear of past experiences and entering into intimacy

Fear of intimacy:

Intimacy means the ability to express your true self genuinely with some other person and compares to the experience of connection and closeness. Some describe various kinds of intimacy, and one or more of them might be embroiled in the terror of it to varying degrees.

Examples are:

- Experiential: The capacity to share interactions with others
- Intellectual: Your ability to communicate with others the opinions and suggestions
- Sexual: The desire to sexually express yourself
- Emotional: The opportunity to communicate with someone the innermost thoughts

The fear of intimacy, though the two may be tightly connected, is different from the fear of vulnerability. At first, or at least even to trustworthy friends and family, a person who lives with the fear of intimacy may be relaxed being vulnerable and exposing their true selves to the world. When a person with anxiety feels certain interactions being too near or intimate, the issue always starts.

Causes of intimacy fear:

For certain people, fears of engulfment and abandonment, and, eventually, fear of loss, are at the core of fear of intimacy, and these 2 fears may sometimes co-exist. While the worries vary significantly from each other, both trigger actions that drag the person in alternate and then drive them away again. In general, these concerns are embedded in past childhood memories and triggered by the present time of adult relationships, which contributes to uncertainty if an individual insists exclusively on evaluating the relationship based on current circumstances.

Fear of being vulnerable or abandonment:

Many that are worried about abandonment feel that they will

be abandoned by their mate. This also results from the trauma of leaving the person physically or emotionally as a young child by a parent or other significant adult figure.

Anxiety disorder:

As part of a social anxiety disorder or social phobia, the fear of contact can also emerge. The fear of intimacy is defined by certain researchers as a subset of these factors. People who risk the evaluation, judgment, or rejection of others are inherently more prone to shy away from forming close, informal relations. Moreover, as part of the fear of intimacy, certain particular phobias, including the fear of touch, can exist. In loose social settings, however, most individuals might be relaxed, numbering their colleagues and social networking contacts in the hundreds, who have no profoundly personal relationships or anything. In fact, since today's technology enables people to disappear behind their mobile phones and social networking, the fear of intimacy can be difficult to target.

Fear of engulfment:

Many who fear engulfment are fearful that in a partnership they would be manipulated, controlled, or lose themselves, and this often derives from having grown up in an enmeshed family.

Major risk factors of fear of intimacy:

Trigger factors for fear of intimacy also derive from childhood and the failure to trust parental figures securely, contributing to difficulties with attachment. Experiences which can cause this involve:

Enmeshed families: Although enmeshed families can tend to be caring and nurturing on the surface, limitations and responsibilities can be blurred and contribute to attachment, in-dependency, and relationship problems.

Parent loss: People who have lost a mother or father through divorce, imprisonment, or death may be left with feelings of rejection and may have a tougher time than adults developing emotional bonds. Research also showed that mental health disorders and resulting distress in intimate relationships are linked with a fear of loss. Research also showed that mental health disorders and resulting distress in intimate relationships are linked with a fear of loss.

Emotional neglect: Parents or caregivers who are physically but not mentally present give the impression to children that they should not be counted on.

Parental illness: A parent's illness may contribute to a feeling of not being able to depend on someone but oneself, particularly where it includes a reversal of role or the need to play a parent and provide for other siblings at an early age.

Parental substance use: Concerns with drug use will make it impossible for parents to have adequate treatment, and can conflict with bond formation.

Verbal abuse: Children that are emotionally exploited can become adults that, if they discuss something with others, risk being mocked or verbally abused, which can contribute to an unwillingness to disclose information and being insecure in relationships with people.

Sexual or physical violence: Childhood abuse may find it impossible as an adult to establish both sexual and emotional intimacy.

Parental mental disease: Evidence shows that parental mental impairment may influence the development of commitment in children, including narcissistic personality disorder, which may contribute to unstable attachment and inadequate coping mechanisms in adulthood.

Neglect: People who have suffered neglect as kids can find it hard to trust and depend on others as adults, even romantic partners.

Signs and Indications:

In any form of relationship, whether romantic, platonic, or family, the fear of intimacy will play out in a variety of different ways. It is important to remember that it is always easy to perceive the signs of an implicit fear of intimacy as the opposite of what the individual is seeking to do in terms of communication. An individual can deeply value close relationships, for example, but their anxiety causes them to do actions that create difficulties to shape and maintain them. Ironically, where the relationship under question is the one that the individual especially enjoys, relationship-sabotaging acts are typically more pronounced. This is especially relevant to consider for those who have been associated with a person dealing with a fear of intimacy. If an individual really longs for closeness, anxiety typically does not cause significant difficulties. Here are several unique and often observed habits.

Fear of commitment and serial dating:

An individual who has this fear of intimacy is always, at least initially, willing to communicate with others. It is as the relationship becomes stronger, as the relationship worth grows, where things start to fall apart. The relationship is broken in some manner, instead of communicating on an emotional basis and substituted by yet another, more shallow relationship. Many short-term relationships are a pattern that is growing. An individual may seem to have commitment phobia or be suspected of being a serial dater for a variety of reasons; fear of intimacy may be one.

Difficulty in expressing your needs:

There can be considerable difficulties for an individual with a fear of intimacy to communicate desires and wishes. Again, these can arise from feeling unworthy of the love of another. Since partners cannot read minds, certain conditions go unfulfilled, effectively confirming the feelings of the individual that they are unworthy. This can develop into a negative circle, one where the lack of awareness of unexpressed desires by a spouse contributes to a greater lack of confidence in the partnership.

Difficulties in developing physical contact:

When you come to physical touch, a fear of intimacy will result in extremes. On the one hand, a person can fully avoid physical contact. They may seem to have a persistent need for physical touch, on the other side.

Coping and management:

There is some study that must be undertaken in order to overcome a fear of intimacy which only you can do, whether you meet with a psychiatrist or not. This mostly comes down to confronting negative attitudes towards oneself and questioning them, which is essential if there is to be a lasting change. This will involve time, a desire to embrace change, and the initiative to learn how and why you created this anxiety through examining your past.

Acceptance for uncertainty:

In the end, those who dread intimacy dread the effects of a relationship that turns sour. The idea that there are no promises in existence or in human relations is necessary to acknowledge. Each relationship with another person is essentially a gamble. Despite this, social experiences remain a central guiding objective of human life. Practicing courage may make a significant difference, and it has been shown that it can alleviate anxiety by creating meaningful relationship interactions. A limitation is that doing something with somebody you feel you can trust is important. Instead of concentrating on a specific consequence, tend to concentrate more on day-to-day life.

Looking at your past:

Most of us may not like to think negatively of a parent, so in an attempt to focus on potential contributors to your avoidance of intimacy, strive to objectively determine your relationships in childhood. Think of your family's messages you got and equate them to the messages they should have given. Knowing that these are not the only examples of relationships will make you understand what might be achievable in forms of intimacy if you had a neglectful, abusive, or engulfing parent.

Looking at your own goals:

In life, what would you really want? Will you want an intimate, long-term relationship? If so, in the past, how did you drive people away? Take time to analyze what your wishes and aspirations were and are and if they are either supported or harmed by your actions.

Give some time to yourself:

It does not happen immediately to resolve a fear of intimacy. You can eventually have failures and though you feel as if you have gained ground. When this arises, offer yourself grace and speak softly to your inner self. In order to have a happier future, strive not to perceive your anxiety as a character defect, but merely something that undoubtedly comes from your distant history that you should work through. Research has also demonstrated that for those who have intimacy difficulties, supportive relationship interactions may be helpful. Getting such meaningful interactions will enhance your capacity over time to build intimacy.

Fear of past experiences:

Any occurrences might have occurred to you and that makes it even more likely that you may feel distressed. History of family, childhood, upbringing, and even genes may play a role. Not everyone is growing up in a household that is always healthy and caring. It might have an effect on your mental well-being later in life if you have a number of recurring traumatic encounters in your childhood. It is well known that challenging situations will contribute to distress in kids and adults in childhood. The likelihood of anxiety and depression may all be raised by experiences like parents breaking up, the loss of a loved partner or friend, substance or alcohol abuse, and money issues. Childhood stress is another major contributing factor for anxiety and depression. The impact may be extreme and long-lasting whether you have seen a member of the family being exploited sexually, physically, or emotionally, or if you are a survivor of violence yourself. The world is likely to be perceived by kids who grow up in violent and dysfunctional setting as an unpredictable, frightening, and sometimes dangerous place. The reaction of rage and frustration, anxiety, and helplessness will persist into adulthood if little is done about it. It's crucial to note that a difficult upbringing is no sure indication that later in life you will develop depression or anxiety. Typically, distress is linked to a variety of variables, and we do have factors that help shield us from the effects of traumatic situations, such as a caring father or close friends. If you think it might be helpful to chat about childhood memories with others, talking about counseling could be the way to go.

Influence of whakapapa and family history:

There is research that suggests that the whakapapa could be inherited or related to an elevated likelihood of anxiety or depression. In families or in relatives, anxiety and depression may be normal. But only because at some point a loving member already has anxiety and depression, does not mean that you always would. There is something you can do to boost your stamina or inner power, particularly though you have a background of anxiety or depression. It's worth looking even deeper than just our grandparents or parents when thinking of our family history and whakapapa. We may still be influenced today by stuff that occurred centuries ago. Without you understanding it, this intergenerational trauma will be passed on and have an influence on your mental well-being today. The lack of land or inequality, for instance, maybe fell down over the centuries. It is crucial to note that your ancestors' abilities are passed on to you as well. Their strength is indeed yours to get it through hardship.

Things you can do to help yourself for feeling better:

You can regulate what you think about things, even though it appears you can't manage your emotions. It is enough to only take a little first step to bring you back on the road of loving life. And if you do not do it alone, it will work so much easier then.

You can talk to someone to get some relief:

Sharing how you feel with someone you know is a safe place to start coping with what's going on. This may be anyone you feel close to in your parents, a friend or your girlfriend, a religious leader, or someone in your culture. It also works if you are not trying to deal on your own with difficult circumstances. Try shifting to your loved ones and mates. Via their affection, respect, warmth, and care, they will provide emotional help and support. They will also encourage you and discuss new and additional information, and also practical assistance, such as finding the stuff you need or assisting with work around the house. You seem to achieve improved physical and emotional well-being if you have strong social reinforcement and find it easy to deal with challenging situations and events.

Things you can do by your own-self:

There are several techniques for self-help that will strengthen all four facets of your life: your social network, your body, your soul, and your mind. The best thing about helping yourself is that you are in control because you can experiment to find what works for you for various methods. You will even get acquainted with peers and loved ones by checking in on how you get on or also performing any of the productive things.

Treatments:

To better cope with the symptoms, it may be advised that you seek medicine or counseling. There are several various forms of therapy and you would be able to pick the best option by learning all about them.

Knowing who can help you:

There are people qualified to assist with anxiety and depression if you need additional support. In face-to-face sessions with health-care professionals, or through calling a helpline, you can receive assistance. Many of these individuals may also have undergone emotional illness because they will appreciate what you are going through. Do not think about calling for support, the quicker the better.

Working with your strengths:

Many people faced shared problems that lead to their interactions with distress. Yet they still have several shared ways to get through the tough periods that enable them to transition to loving life again.

Chapter 03: Major types of Anxiety and Anxiety management

This chapter covers all the major types of anxiety in detail. Symptoms, causes and strategies to overcome generalized anxiety disorder and post traumatic anxiety disorder are mentioned in this chapter. What are obsessions and compulsions, why people have them and how to cope up with this disorder are also mentioned. How to deal or prevent social anxiety and what causes it, common phobias that people have, all are the significant aspects of the given chapter. Most useful anxiety management strategies are also part of this chapter

3.1 Generalized Anxiety Disorder

Feeling anxious and stressed from time to time is common, particularly if your life is challenging. However, a symptom of generalized anxiety disorder may be excessive, persistent anxiety, and concern that are difficult to manage and interfere with daily tasks. As an infant or an adult, it is likely to experience a generalized anxiety disorder. There are signs of generalized anxiety disorder that are identical to panic disorder, obsessive-compulsive disorder, and other anxiety forms, yet these are also distinct disorders. Living with a generalized anxiety disorder may be a struggle in the long run. It happens associated with other mood or anxiety problems in many situations. With medications or psychotherapy, severe anxiety disorder progresses in most situations. It may help to develop coping strategies, create lifestyle changes, and use calming techniques.

Signs and symptoms:

A sign of generalized anxiety disorder may differ. They can contain:

- Persistent fear or anxiety over a variety of areas that are out of comparison to the result of the accidents
- Difficulty in concentration, or the sense that the mind goes blank
- Perceiving circumstances and incidents as harmful, even though they are not
- Overthinking solutions and plans to all potential worst-case results
- Trouble managing confusion

- Failure to put worry aside or let go
- Fear and indecisiveness of making the incorrect option
- Feeling nervous, unwilling to sleep, and feeling up or on the edge of the key

Physical symptoms and signs can include:

- Tiredness
- Muscle ache or muscle tension
- Irritability
- Sleep problems
- Feeling twitchy or trembling
- Sweating
- Nervousness or getting startled quickly
- Diarrhea, nausea, or condition with irritable bowel

There might be occasions where you are not totally overwhelmed by your fears, but even when there is no clear cause, you always feel nervous. You may have deep fear about your welfare or that of your family members, for instance, or you could have a general feeling that something terrible is going to happen. In social, job, or other aspects of your life, physical signs, anxiety, or concern trigger your considerable distress. Worries can change from one issue to another, and over time and maturity, they can change.

Symptoms in teenagers and children:

Children and teens may have common issues to those of adults, but may also have excessive concerns about:

- School results or sports activities
- Being on time or punctuality
- Security of family members
- Nuclear war, other catastrophic events or earthquakes

A child or teenager with extreme anxiety can:

- Sound overly eager to blend in.
- Redoing activities because the first time they are not fine
- Wants to be a perfectionist
- Excessive time spent on homework
- Lack of confidence
- Strive for consent
- Needs a lot of reassurance regarding progress
- Avoid attending college or preventing social conditions

Have regular stomachaches or other medical problems

Seeing for a doctor:

It is common to have any anxiety but see your doctor if:

- You sound like you are thinking so hard, whether your career, relationships, or other aspects of your life are messing with it.
- Have suicidal feelings or actions, then obtain urgent medical care
- You feel sad or irritable, you have issues with medications or alcohol, or you have some questions regarding mental well being and anxiety.

It is doubtful that the problems would necessarily go away by itself, and they may potentially become worse with time. Before the distress gets severe, it might be better to handle it early on. Continue to get professional help.

Causes of GAD:

The origin of generalized anxiety disorder, as with many mental health disorders, possibly derives from a dynamic interaction of environmental and biological causes, which may include:

- Brain Chemistry and Work Variations

- Personality and development
- Differences in the manner in which risks are seen
- Genes

Predisposing factors:

Women are far more commonly afflicted with a generalized anxiety disorder than men are. The chances of having a generalized anxiety disorder can be raised by the following factors:

Individuality. A person whose disposition is timid or pessimistic or who refuses something risky may be more susceptible than others to generalized anxiety disorder.

Experiences. People with a generalized anxiety disorder may have a childhood memory that is stressful or negative, a history of major changes in life, or a recent negative traumatic occurrence. The likelihood may be elevated by serious medical conditions or other mental health problems.

Genes. In families, a generalized anxiety disorder can be present.

Hurdles or complications of GAD can cause:

It may be disabling to have a generalized anxiety disorder. It is capable of:

- Impair the capacity to rapidly and accurately execute activities when you have difficulty focusing
- Draining up your energy
- Take focus and time from other activities,
- Raising the possibility of depression

Other physical health problems may often result in or intensify generalized anxiety disorder, such as:

- Heart-health problems
- Problems of stomach or intestinal disorders, such as or ulcer irritable bowel syndrome
- Chronic illness and pain
- Migraines and Headaches
- Trouble in sleep and insomnia

Along with like most mental health disorders, generalized anxiety disorder also exists, and may render diagnosis and recovery more difficult. Such frequently occurring mental health problems including generalized anxiety disorder include:

- Phobia
- Depression

- (PTSD) Post-traumatic stress disorder
- Obsessive-compulsive disorder (OCD)
- Suicide or suicidal thoughts
- Drug abuse

Preventive measures:

There is no way to say for certain what would lead anyone to develop a generalized anxiety disorder, so if you have anxiety, you should take action to reduce the effect of symptoms:

Get early help. If you hesitate, anxiety will be harder to treat, as many mental health problems

In your life, prioritize problems. By good control of your time and resources, you will reduce anxiety.

Keep a diary. Trying to keep track of your private life will help you and your therapist to understand what makes you stress and what appears to help you feel happier.

Stop unhealthy drug use. Anxiety may be induced or exacerbated by alcohol and drug usage and also caffeine or nicotine usage. If you are hooked to either of these compounds, it will make you nervous to quit. See a psychiatrist or locate a recovery facility or help group to assist you if you cannot leave on your own.

3.2 Post-Traumatic Anxiety or stress disorder

(PTSD) Post-traumatic stress disorder is a mental health problem that is caused either by suffering or watching a terrifying occurrence. Symptoms, and also some uncontrollable feelings regarding the incident, can involve hallucinations, extreme distress, and nightmares. Many persons who go through stressful experiences can have temporary trouble adapting and managing, but they typically get stronger over time and proper self-care. You could have PTSD if the effects get worse, persist for months or years, and interact with the day-to-day functioning. To minimize symptoms and increase function, having appropriate care during the emergence of PTSD symptoms may be crucial.

Signs and symptoms:

Symptoms of post-traumatic stress disorder can begin within one month after a traumatic experience, but symptoms may not occur until years after the incident, often. In work or social conditions and in marriages, these signs trigger critical difficulties. They can even mess with your willingness to perform your everyday activities normally. Symptoms of PTSD are commonly classified into four types: recurring memories, pessimistic shifts of attitude and thought, avoidance, and shifts of emotional and physical pain. Symptoms may differ with time or vary from individual to individual.

Intruding memories:

Intruding or intrusive memory signs can include:

- Unwanted recurrent unpleasant memories of the traumatic incident
- Upsetting visions or nightmares about a painful experience
- Reliving the painful experience as if it were occurring (flashbacks) again

- Extreme psychiatric illness or bodily responses to something that triggers you of a painful experience

Negative changes in mood and thinking:

Symptoms of harmful changes in perception and attitude may involve:

- Difficulty having positive thoughts
- Negative feelings regarding yourself, the world, or other people
- Problems in a recall, like not recalling major details of the stressful experience
- Hopelessness regarding the future
- Feeling separated from friends and relatives
- Difficulty in keeping strong relations
- Lack of motivation you once enjoyed in things
- Feeling numb emotionally

Avoidance:

Avoidance signs can include:

- Avoiding events, sites, or persons that remind you of a traumatic experience
- Trying not to remember or speak about the painful experience

Changes in emotional and physical reactions:

Symptoms of improvements (also termed as arousal symptoms) in emotional and physical pain can include:

- Easily startled or terrified
- Concentrating difficulty
- Self-destructive actions, such as over-drinking or moving too rapidly
- Being always on guard for danger
- Sleeping Trouble
- Irritability, aggressive behavior, or angry outbursts
- Overwhelming shame or guilt

Symptoms and signs can also contain the following for children six years old and younger:

- Scary visions that may or may not contain components of a stressful experience
- Re-enacting, by play, the traumatic incident or facets of the traumatic experience

The intensity of signs and symptoms:

Symptoms of PTSD can differ in severity over time. When you're depressed in general, or even when you run across memories about what you passed through, you might experience more PTSD signs. You can, for instance, hear a car backfire and then relive fighting experiences. Or you might see an article of a sexual attack on the television and feel overwhelmed by your own attack experiences.

Seeing a doctor:

Speak to a psychiatrist or a mental health specialist whether you have troubling thoughts and emotions regarding a traumatic experience after longer than a month, if they are serious, or whether you find you are having difficulty keeping a life back under control. Seeking care as quickly as possible will help avoid the effects of PTSD from deteriorating.

If you have suicidal thoughts or someone you know, seek treatment right away from one or more of such resources:

- Talk to a mate or loved one who is near.
- To contact a trained counselor, dial the number of a suicide hotline. Using the appropriate number and click them to hit the lines that offer assistance.
- In your religious culture, meet a church leader, a pastor, or someone.
- Create an appointment with a mental health specialist or a psychiatrist.

Getting emergency help:

Dial 911 or your nearest emergency line instantly if you suspect you could injure yourself or try suicide. When you meet someone who is at risk of wanting to commit suicide or has tried to commit suicide, make sure that someone sticks with that individual to keep him or her safe. Immediately dial 911 or the nearest emergency number. Or send the individual to the nearby hospital emergency department, if you can do so safely.

Causes and reasons:

When you see, go through or learn of an incident causing real or threatened death, severe injury, or sexual violation, you may experience post-traumatic stress disorder. Doctors are not sure whether they get PTSD in other people. PTSD is typically induced, as with most mental health disorders, by a dynamic combination of:

- Stressful interactions, such as the number and intensity of pain that you have encountered in your life
- Inherited traits of your character, also referred to as your temperament
- Inherited threats to mental wellbeings, such as a personal history of anxiety and depression

- The way your brain controls the chemicals and hormones produced by your body in reaction to stress

Risk factors:

Post-traumatic stress disorder may happen to people of all ages. However, following a traumatic incident, certain factors can make a person more likely to develop PTSD, such as:

- Experiencing severe or sustained injuries
- Doing a role that raises the likelihood of adverse accidents, such as military staff and first responders
- Having endured other early in life trauma, such as childhood abuse
- Getting other difficulties of mental wellbeings, such as depression or anxiety
- Lack of a strong system of care for family and friends
- Having alcohol abuse issues, such as binge consumption or drug usage,
- Having blood relatives with any mental health challenges, including depression or anxiety

Forms of traumatic events:

The most prevalent incidents contributing to PTSD development include:

- Exposure of Combat
- Being targeted with a pistol
- Sexual harassment
- Physical abuse in childhood
- Physical violence
- An incident

PTSD may also contribute to numerous other stressful incidents, such as fire, natural disaster, terrorist attack, mugging, robbery, torture, plane crash, life-threatening medical condition, kidnapping, among other incidents that are serious or life-threatening.

Complications in PTSD:

Post-traumatic stress disorder may interfere with your life, career, wellbeing, relationships, and the enjoyment of daily activities.

Getting PTSD will also raise the likelihood of other issues with mental well-beings, such as:

- Anxiety and depression
- Disorders of eating
- Issues of consuming narcotics or drink

- Suicidal ideas and actions

Preventive measures:

Some individuals have PTSD-like effects at first after experiencing a stressful incident, such as unable to avoid worrying about what is happened. Both of these are normal responses to trauma: terror, rage, anxiety, depression, shame. The majority of trauma-exposed patients, though, do not experience post-traumatic stress disorder for a long time. It may avoid natural stress reactions from becoming worse and progressing into PTSD by obtaining timely aid and support. This may suggest turning to friends and relatives who can listen and give support. For a short course in treatment, it can involve finding out a mental health specialist. Any persons will also find it useful to shift to their communities of faith. Help from others can often help deter you from shifting to harmful ways of coping, such as alcohol or drug consumption.

3.3 Obsessive-Compulsive Disorder

The obsessive-compulsive disorder also known as OCD has a history of unwanted feelings and worries (obsessions) that contribute to repeated (compulsive) activities. Such compulsions and obsessions interfere with day-to-day tasks and trigger major anxiety. You can attempt to disregard your obsessions or avoid them, but that just raises your depression and anxiety. Ultimately, in order to attempt to relieve the discomfort, you feel compelled to commit compulsive actions. They keep on coming back despite attempts to ignore or to get rid of worrisome feelings or impulses. This, the vicious circle of OCD, contributes to more ritualistic actions. OCD also circles around such subjects, such as the irrational apprehension of germ exposure. To relieve your fears of infection, you can wash your hands compulsively until they are sore and chapped. You may be embarrassed and ashamed about the disorder if you have OCD, but therapy may be successful.

Signs and symptoms:

The obsessive-compulsive disorder typically encompasses compulsions as well as obsessions. But you can also only have symptoms of obsession or just symptoms of compulsion. You may or may not know that your compulsions and obsession are irrational or excessive, but they consume a lot of time and disrupt with the operation of your everyday life and social, education, or job.

Obsession symptoms:

Unwanted, repeated, and intense feelings, desires, or images that are distracting and causing panic or anxiety are OCD obsessions. By doing a compulsive activity or ritual, you may attempt to avoid them or to get rid of them. When you're attempting to conceive about or do other stuff, these obsessions usually intrude.

Obsessions provide themes with them sometimes, such as:

- Fear of dirt or contamination
- Unwanted feelings, like violence, or topics of sex or faith
- Needing tidy and symmetrical things
- Doubting and experiencing problems tolerating misunderstanding
- Violent or horrible feelings of losing power and hurting oneself or anyone.

Examples of the symptoms and signs of obsession include:

- Fear of being infected by handling items touched by others
- Extreme tension when objects are not orderly or in any way facing

- Doubts that you have the door closed or the stove switched off
- Pictures of driving a vehicle through a mass of individuals
- Uncomfortable sexual videos
- Thoughts on yelling obscenities or inappropriately behaving in public
- Avoidance of conditions which may trigger obsessions, like trembling hands

Compulsion symptoms:

Repetitive habits that you are compelled to continue are OCD compulsions. This repeated habits or behavioral actions are supposed to relieve discomfort or avoid something unpleasant from occurring linked to your obsessions. Participating in the compulsions, though, provides little gratification and can only provide brief relief from anxiety. When you are experiencing obsessive feelings, you might think up guidelines or habits to obey to help regulate your anxiety. These compulsions are unhealthy and are sometimes not really connected to the issue they are supposed to address.

Compulsions, as with obsessions, usually include themes, such as:

- Cleaning and washing
- Following a strict schedule
- Counting
- Checking
- Orderliness
- Demanding for reassurance

Examples of signs and effects of compulsion include:

- Washing your hands until you have raw skin
- Repeating a word, prayer, or phrase quietly
- Repeatedly testing the stove to ensure that it is off
- Repeatedly locking doors to ensure they're closed
- Counting In particular patterns
- Arrange the canned food in the same way to face the same

Variety in severity:

In the adolescent or young adult years, OCD typically starts, although it may begin in childhood. Symptoms typically begin progressively and across life appear to differ in intensity. Over time, the kinds of compulsions and obsessions that you encounter will also shift. When you undergo greater discomfort, symptoms usually worsen. OCD may have mild to moderate effects, typically called a lifelong condition, or it may be so extreme and time-intensive that it has become disabling.

Seeing a doctor:

There's a contrast between becoming a perfectionist, somebody who, for example, expects ideal outcomes or results, and possessing OCD. OCD concerns are not necessarily excessive fears over real issues in your life or having to clean or plan stuff in a certain way. See a psychiatrist or mental health specialist whether compulsions and obsessions are impacting your standard of living.

Causes and reasons:

There is not a full explanation of the origin of obsessive-compulsive disorder. Among the key hypotheses are:

Biology. OCD may be a consequence of changes in the normal chemistry or cognitive functions of your body itself.

Learning. Obsessive thoughts and compulsive habits may be acquired or eventually learned over time by observing family members.

Genetics. OCD may have a genetic aspect, but it has yet to define individual genes.

Predisposing factors of OCD:

Factors that can raise the likelihood of obsessive-compulsive disorder developing or causing it include:

- History of families. Getting parents with the disease or other family members may raise the chance of developing OCD.
- Other disorders in mental wellbeing. OCD can be correlated with other problems in mental wellbeings, such as depressive disorders, anxiety, tic disorders, or drug misuse.
- Stressful things throughout life. Your chance can increase if you've undergone stressful or traumatic events. For some cause, this reaction can activate the repetitive rituals, thoughts, and emotional disturbance that characterize OCD.

Issues or complications:

Problems that arise from the obsessive-compulsive disorder can include:

- Excessive time spent practicing ritualistic actions
- Low quality of life generally
- Difficulty attending jobs, social gatherings, or school

- Health conditions, like contact dermatitis from excessive washing of hands
- Troubled friendships
- Suicidal thinking and actions

Preventive measures:

There are no definitive means of preventing obsessive-compulsive disorder. Having care as quickly as possible, though, will help avoid OCD from worsening and upsetting habits and the everyday life.

3.4 Social Anxiety

In certain social settings, it's natural to feel anxious. For instance, the sensation of butterflies in the stomach may be triggered by going on a date or making a presentation. Yet daily encounters induce substantial distress, fear, self-consciousness, and embarrassment in social anxiety disorder, often called social phobia, since your paranoia being scrutinized or evaluated by others. Anxiety and fear in social anxiety disorder contribute to avoidance that may ruin your life. Your everyday life, career, education, or other hobbies may be influenced by extreme stress. A persistent mental health problem is a generalized anxiety disorder but developing coping strategies through psychotherapy and getting medications will help you build confidence and strengthen the capacity to communicate with others.

Signs and symptoms:

Feelings of discomfort or shyness in some environments, particularly in children, are not usually symptoms of social anxiety disorder. Based on individual qualities and life experiences, trust levels in social settings differ. Naturally, certain persons are quiet while others are more outgoing. Social anxiety disorder, in comparison to ordinary nervousness, involves anxiety, paranoia, and isolation that interfere with regular life, work, education, or other hobbies. Usually, social anxiety disorder starts in the early to mid-teens, but it may also begin in younger kids or in adults.

Physical signs and symptoms:

A social anxiety disorder may also be followed by physical signs and symptoms and can include:

- Blushing
- Tremble
- Heart beating fast
- Transpiration
- Difficulties holding your breath
- Tension in the muscles
- Lightheadedness or dizziness

- Stomach upset or nausea
- Feeling your mind's gone blank

Behavioral and emotional symptoms:

Persistent symptoms or signs of social anxiety disorder may include:

- Fear in circumstances where you may be criticized
- Intense fear of engaging with outsiders or communicating with them
- Worrying of yourself being ashamed or insulted
- Expecting the worst potential outcomes during a social situation from a negative event
- Fear of someone thinking that you appear anxious
- To stop doing stuff or communicating to persons out of fear of humiliation
- Fear of physical signs such as blushing, shaking, sweating, or hearing a shaky voice that may cause you humiliation
- Avoiding scenarios where you may be the object of attention
- Or extreme fear or distress, experiencing a social condition

- In preparation for a feared event or occurrence, possessing anxiety
- Spending time assessing your results and finding weaknesses in your relationships after a social scenario

Anxiety about communicating with adults or peers can be shown in children by screaming, throwing temper tantrums, sticking to parents, or declining to speak in social settings.

Social anxiety disorder performance type is where you feel extreme fear and anxiety only while public speaking or acting, but not in any kind of social circumstances.

Showing avoidance of common social situations:

For instance, normal, daily encounters that can be difficult to bear when you have a social anxiety disorder usually include:

- Interacting with unknown persons or outsiders
- Going to school or job
- Attending social events or parties
- Begin discussions
- Dating
- Creating eye contact
- Entering a space where people are already sitting

- Eating in the company of someone
- Returning things to a supermarket
- Using a public bathroom

Symptoms or signs of social anxiety disorder may shift with time. If you are under a lot of stress or demands, they can flare-up. While preventing conditions that cause anxiety may help you feel comfortable in the short term, if you don't get care, the anxiety is likely to persist throughout the long term.

Seeing for a doctor:

If you dread and avoid regular social interactions because they induce worry, embarrassment, or panic, see your physician or mental health provider.

Reasons and causes:

Social anxiety disorder, like many other behavioral health disorders, typically results from a dynamic interaction between environmental and biological causes. Causes that are possible include:

Traits inherited. Disorders of anxiety appear to run in households. However, how much of this could be attributed to genetics or how much is attributed to acquired behavior is not completely clear.

Environment. Environment Social anxiety disorder can be a learned trait, and during an uncomfortable or awkward social event, certain individuals can experience the problem. There may also be a relationship between social anxiety disorder and the parents who either represent anxious behavior in social circumstances or their children are more controlled or overprotective.

Brain structure. In regulating the fear response, a structure in your brain called the amygdala can play a role. People who have a hyperactive amygdala can have an intensified reaction to fear, which in social environments causes increased anxiety.

Risk causing factors:

The likelihood of having social anxiety disorder may be raised by many causes, including:

- History of families. If your siblings or biological parents have the disease, you are more likely to have a social anxiety disorder.
- Having an appearance or state that attracts attention. Stuttering, facial disfigurement, or tremors related to Parkinson's disease, for example, can intensify feelings of self-consciousness and can cause certain people's social anxiety disorder.

- Temperament. Children who, when meeting new circumstances or individuals, are withdrawn, shy, timid, or restrained can be in greater danger.
- Negative experiences. It may be more likely to social anxiety disorder with children who encounter bullying, teasing, rejection, ridicule, or humiliation. Furthermore, a social anxiety disorder can be linked with other traumatic incidents in life, like family conflict, violence, or trauma.
- New demands for culture or work. Symptoms of social anxiety disorder usually begin in the teenage years, however for the first time, meeting new people, delivering a speech in public, or having an essential job presentation may cause symptoms.

Hurdles and complications:

Social anxiety disorder will run your life if it is left untreated. Job, education, relationships, or the pleasure of life may conflict with anxieties. A disorder of social anxiety can cause:

- Low self-esteem for oneself
- Hypersensitivity to criticism
- Trouble with being forceful
- Isolation and difficult relationships in society

- Impaired social skills
- Poor achievement in academics and work
- Attempts to commit suicide
- Abuse of substances, like drinking too much alcohol

Social anxiety disorder also correlates with other anxiety disorders and other mental conditions, especially substance abuse and major depressive disorder

Preventive measures:

There is no way of predicting what will cause somebody to develop the anxiety disorder, but if you are anxious, you can take steps to decrease the impact of symptoms:

Get early help. If you wait, anxiety can be harder to treat, like many mental health conditions.

In your life, prioritize problems. By good control of your time and resources, you will reduce anxiety. Make sure you invest time doing stuff that you love.

Keep a journal. Trying to keep track of the private life can help you determine what causes you stress and it seems to make you feel better, your health care professional.

Avoid unhealthy drug use. Anxiety can be caused or worsened by drug and alcohol use and even nicotine or caffeine use. If you are addicted to either of these compounds, it will make you nervous to quit. See a psychiatrist or find a recovery facility or help network to assist you if you cannot leave on your own.

3.5 Disorder Phobias

An irrational fear of anything that is unlikely to cause damage is a phobia. The word itself comes from Phobos, a Greek word meaning fear or horror. For instance, hydrophobia simply translates to fear of water. They feel an extreme fear of a particular entity or circumstance when someone has a phobia. As they trigger severe anxiety, phobias are distinct from normal fears, likely interfering with life at home, job, or schooling. People with phobias are deliberately ignoring or experiencing the phobic entity or disorder with extreme fear or anxiety. A type of anxiety condition is phobias. There are very common anxiety conditions. For any point in their life, they are expected to impact more than 30 percent of adults. The American Psychiatric Association describes several of the common phobias in the Diagnostic and Statistical Manual of Mental Disorders, Fifth Edition (DSM-5).

With its own special diagnoses, agoraphobia, a fear of situations or places that cause helplessness or fear, is pointed out as an especially common fear. With a special condition, social phobias, which are concerns connected with social environments, are often singled out. A broad classification of unique phobias related to particular objects and situations are specific phobias. Approximate 12.5 percent of adults are influenced by specific phobias. Phobias come in any size and form. The list of specific phobias is very long because there is an infinite number of situations or objects. Usually, unique phobias come into five broad categories:

- Blood, injuries, or medical complications (injections, accidents, fractured bones) related fears
- Natural environment-related concerns (heights, darkness, thunder)
- Specific situation-related fears (flying, driving, riding an elevator)
- Animal-based fears (spiders, snakes, dogs)
- Other fears (choking, drowning, noisy sounds)

When they are in such situations, individuals with anxiety problems often have panic attacks. These panic attacks can be really uncomfortable that in the future, individuals may try all they can do to stop them. If you experience a panic attack when sailing, for example, those categories comprise an unlimited number of particular items and conditions. Other than what is described in the DSM, there's not an official phobia list, but practitioners and experts think up terms for them as the need occurs. Typically, this is done by merging a Greek (or Latin) prefix describing the phobia with the suffix of -phobia.

For instance, mixing hydro (water) & phobia (fear) will be considered a fear of water. There's something like a fear of fear (photophobia) as well. In fact, this is more usual than you would think. In the future, you may fear sailing, but you may also be afraid of panic attacks or afraid of developing hydro-phobia.

List of some most common phobias:

It is a complex method to analyze specific phobias. For these conditions, most individuals do not seek treatment, so cases majorly go unreported. Based on some cultural experiences, gender, and age, these phobias often differ. Some of the phobias that are most common include:

- Acrophobia, height fear
- Arachnophobia, spider's fear

- Aerophobia, flying fear
- Astraphobia, fear of lightning and thunder
- Autophobia that is fear about being alone
- Hemophobia, blood fears
- Claustrophobia, fear of restricted or crowded spaces
- Ophidiophobia, fear about snakes
- Hydrophobia, water fear
- Zoophobia, animal fear

List of some unique or unusual phobias:

Specific phobias are often incredibly specific. Some are so much so that only a few individuals may be impacted at a time. These are impossible to recognize and most patients do not disclose to the clinicians, their unusual fears. Some of the more uncommon phobias include examples of:

- Cryophobia, ice or cold fear
- Fear of chickens, Alektorophobia
- Fear of beards, Pogonophobia
- Onomatophobia, fear about names
- Nephophobia, cloud fear

Specific phobias are an unreasonable and overwhelming fear of objects or circumstances that pose a slight real danger but cause anxiety and avoidance. Specific phobias are long-lasting, produce extreme psychologically and physically responses, and may impact the ability to perform normally at job, in social environments, or at school, unlike the slight fear that you can have while delivering a speech or taking an exam. Among the most popular anxiety disorders are specific phobias, and not all phobias require treatment. But if your everyday life is impaired by a single phobia, many treatments are accessible that will help you move past your worries to resolve them, even forever.

Signs and symptoms:

Severe, recurring fear of a certain object or circumstance that is out of proportion to the real danger includes a particular phobia. There are several forms of phobias, and having a single phobia over more than one object or circumstance is not uncommon. Along with many other forms of anxiety disorders, specific phobias can also happen. Fear of the common examples of specific phobias are:

- Situations such as aero-planes, small areas, or school trips
- Insects or animals, including dogs or spiders

- Nature, such as thunderstorms or heights
- Others, like choking, vomiting, loud noises, clowns, etc.
- Blood, accident, or injection, such as burns, needles, or surgical procedures

A single phobia is related to by its own name. Acrophobia for the height fear and claustrophobia is the fear of enclosed spaces are instances of more general terms. It is likely to produce such types of reactions no matter what particular phobia you have:

- When exposed to and even beginning to think about the origin of your fear, an instant feeling of intense anxiety, fear, and panic
- Worsening anxiety when the circumstance or entity in duration or physical proximity gets near to you
- Feeling dizzy, feeling nauseated, fainting with scars or blood
- Knowing that your worries are irrational or exaggerated, but feeling incapable of managing them
- Doing all possible to avoid or endure the situations or object with intense fear or anxiety

- Physical responses and sensations, such as sweating, quick heartbeat, shortness of breath, or tight chest
- Normally, difficulty functioning because of ones fear
- In kids, maybe tantrums, crying, clinging, or turning down the side of a parent or approach their fear

Seeking a doctor:

For example, an unreasonable fear may be an irritation, having to take stairs rather than an elevator or driving long way to work rather than taking the freeway, but unless it severely disrupts your life, it is not considered as a specific phobia. If anxiety adversely impacts coping at work, school, or social settings, speak with the psychiatrist or a mental health provider. Childhood fears are common, such as fear of monsters, of dark, or being left alone, and they are outgrown by most children. But if a child has chronic, unreasonable anxiety that interferes with day-to-day home or school life, speak to your child's psychiatrist. With the right therapy, most individuals can be helped. And when the phobia is discussed right away instead of waiting, therapy means that it is easier.

Reasons or causes:

Much about the real cause of the specific phobias is still unknown. The following can be the causes:

- Negative experiences. As a consequence of experiencing a traumatic encounter or panic reaction linked to a single object or circumstance, several phobias grow.

- Function of the Brain. In forming particular phobias, differences in brain structure can also play a part.
- Environment and Genetics. There might be a link to your specific phobia and your parents' phobia or fear, which may be due to learned behavior or genetics.

Predisposing factors:

Your likelihood of specific phobias can increase with these variables:

- Your age. In childhood, specific phobias may first arise, typically around age 10, but can develop later in life.
- Temperament of yours. If you are more sensitive, inhibited, or more pessimistic than the standard, your risk can increase.
- Learning from negative encounters. Hearing the negative evidence or experiences, like plane accidents, may contribute to a particular phobia being developed.
- Relatives of yours. You are more prone to experience it, too, if anyone in the family has a particular phobia or fear. This may be a hereditary trait, whether through watching the phobic response of a family member to an object or a circumstance, children can develop particular phobias.

- Negative experience. The emergence of a particular phobia may be caused by witnessing a terrifying stressful experience, such as getting stuck in an elevator or assaulted by an animal.

Hurdles and complications:

While particular phobias can sound dumb to some, they may be harmful to the persons that have them, creating issues that affect multiple facets of life.

- Social separation. Professional, academic, and relationship difficulties may be triggered by avoiding locations and things you dread. Kids with these disabilities are at risk of learning difficulties and loneliness, and if their activities vary greatly from their peers, they can have difficulty with social skills.
- Suicide. Any persons having specific phobias could be at risk of committing suicide.
- Drug abuse. The burden of living with a particularly severe phobia can contribute to drug or alcohol dependence.
- Disorders of mood. Most patients have depression like many other anxiety conditions and unique phobias.

Preventive measures:

If you have a particular phobia, consider having psychological assistance, particularly if you have kids. While genetics is likely to play a role in the creation of individual phobias, witnessing the phobic response of someone else frequently will cause a particular phobia in children. You will teach your child outstanding resilience skills when living with your own worries, and inspire her or him to take brave steps just as you did.

3.6 Anxiety management strategies

There are ways for the fear to calm. In reaction to a difficult situation, recognize the sensation of your heart pounding faster. Or maybe, instead, when you are faced with an overwhelming challenge or case, the palms get sweaty. That is fear, the innate reaction of our body to stress. If the causes have not yet been found, below are a few popular ones: the first day at a new workplace, meeting the family of your wife or making a talk in front of a number of people. Everybody has multiple causes, and one of the most crucial factors in dealing with and controlling anxiety attacks is to recognize them. It will take some time and reflection of your own self to recognize the causes. There are items you should do in the meanwhile and continue to either relax or silence the fear from taking over.

Some effective ways to cope up with anxiety:

There are many quick natural solutions that might help you gain care of the problem if the distress is intermittent and standing in the way of the concentration or activities. If your anxiety is centered on a circumstance, such as being concerned about an event planned, you may notice the side effects are short-lived and low mileage after the expected event occurs.

The practice of having deep and focused breathing:

Try 4 counts of breathing in and 4 counts of breathing out for a total of 5 minutes. You slow your pulse rate by evening out the breath, which can help settle you down. Anxiety is often considered to be improved by the 4-7-8 form.

Doing yoga or going for a walk:

Often, getting away from the problem is the only approach to avoid nervous feelings. It could help alleviate your anxiety by taking some time to reflect not on your mind but your body.

Questioning your own pattern of thoughts:

In your head, negative feelings will take hold and misrepresent the seriousness of the problem. One approach is to doubt your fears, ask whether they are real, and see if you can gain care of them.

Using aromatherapy:

Scents like lavender, chamomile, and sandalwood can be really calming, whether they are in oil shape, incense, or a candle. It is believed that aromatherapy helps stimulate certain receptors in the brain, possibly alleviating anxiety.

Writing down your own thoughts:

It takes it out of your mind to write down what makes you nervous, which will make it less overwhelming. These tricks of calming are particularly effective for those who sporadically feel anxiety. When they are in a dilemma, they can also work well on someone who has GAD (generalized anxiety disorder). However, if you suspect that you have GAD, the only kind of medication you use need not be easy coping mechanisms. To further mitigate the duration of symptoms and also keep them from occurring, you will want to find long-term solutions.

Few long-term anxiety coping strategies:

If anxiety is a daily part of your life, to help you hold it in control, it is crucial to find recovery methods. It could be a mixture of things, such as yoga and talk therapy, or it could only be a case of taking away or overcoming the cause for the fear. If you are not sure where to proceed, exploring solutions with mental health specialists who may consider something that you have not thought about before is always beneficial.

Keep your mind and body healthy:

Regularly exercising, having adequate sleep, consuming healthy food, and remaining involved with those who care for you are perfect strategies to avoid the effects of anxiety.

Knowing how to manage your own triggers:

On your own or through a therapist, you can recognize causes. They can be noticeable often, like smoking, caffeine, or consuming alcohol. They can be much less noticeable at some moments. It takes some time for long-term issues, such as work or financial-related circumstances, to find out, whether it is a due date, the situation, or a person. This may include any additional assistance, by counseling or through friends.

So if you work the cause out, if you may, you can aim to restrict the exposure. Using some coping strategies can improve if you cannot restrict it, as if it is due to a difficult job atmosphere that you cannot currently alter.

The following are several general triggers:

- A career or work atmosphere that is frustrating
- In your family, genetics could trigger anxiety.
- To drive or fly
- Withdrawal from prescriptions or certain substances
- Caffeine
- Trauma
- Side effects of some medicines
- Some phobias, like agoraphobia (open or crowded spaces fear) and also claustrophobia (small spaces fear)
- Chronic distress
- Any chronic conditions, such as diabetes, asthma, or heart disease.
- Having another psychiatric disorder or anxiety

Doing meditation in your routine:

Although this requires some time to achieve effectively, when practiced daily, mindfulness meditation will effectively help you teach your brain to reject anxious feelings when they emerge. Try beginning with yoga if it is tough to sit still and focus.

Adapting cognitive-behavioral therapy (CBT):

CBT lets individuals develop various ways of reasoning about and adapting to circumstances that induce distress. Before spiraling, a psychiatrist will help you develop methods of improving negative thinking processes and attitudes.

Try to change your diet or supplements:

It is certainly a long-term policy to change your lifestyle or take supplements. Research suggests certain vitamins or nutrients can improve anxiety prevention. They include:

- Balm of Lemon
- Ashwagandha
- Fatty Fats omega-3
- Green tea
- Kava kava
- Root of Valerian

- (in moderation) Dark Chocolate

It can take up to 3 months, though, until the body actually works on the nutrients supplied by these herbs and foods. When you are taking any drugs, make sure to explore natural treatments with the doctor.

Ask for your medications to your doctor:

Depending on your signs, if your anxiety is serious enough that the mental health provider feels you'd profit from treatment, there are a variety of places to go. Discuss your issues with your psychiatrist.

When anxiety can be harmful?

It can be very difficult to determine what type of anxiety you are coping with and how one's body responds to potential threat can be radically different relative to another person. It is possible that you have heard anxiety as a general word for the feeling of nervousness generally, worry, or unease. In reaction to an impending experience that has an unpredictable result, it is always a feeling developed. At one time or the other, every individual deals with it, and it is part of the reaction of our brain to a potential threat, even though that threat is not true. There are moments when anxiety may get intense and develop into even anxiety attacks that briefly sound manageable and then steadily build up within a few hours.

(This is distinct from just a panic attack, which subsides and is out of the blue.)

Chapter 04: Anxiety in a relationship

What does anxiety in relationship means and how to recognize it, how to understand insecurity and what are its signs, are all the major concern of this chapter. What is jealousy in relationships and how to build trust in couples is also mentioned. How to eliminate negative thinking and fear of abandonment, how to resolve conflicts and save your relationship are also given in this chapter in detail. Some golden rules to live a very happy and healthy life in a relationship is also the main concern of this chapter.

4.1 What is anxiety in relationships and how to recognize it?

You are in a relationship with somebody you enjoy who is a wonderful guy. You have developed limits, trust, and learned the communication styles of each other. At the same time, you could find yourself continually challenging your mate, you, and the relationship. Are things going to last? And what if they hide a hidden secret? How would you know if this individual really is the right person for you? What if you are actually unable to sustain a safe, devoted relationship? There is a term for this persistent worry: relationship anxiety. It applies to certain feelings of confusion, fear, and doubt that may arise in such relationships, even though all is going reasonably well. Anxiety regarding relationships is exceedingly normal. During the beginning of a relationship, certain persons feel relationship distress, until they realize their spouse has an equivalent interest in them. Or, whether they even want to get in a relationship, they may be uncertain. Although in dedicated, long-term marriages, these emotions will often occur. Over time, anxiety in relationships can result in:

- Emotional discomfort
- A disturbed stomach and other physical problems
- Exhaustion or emotional fatigue
- Absence of motivation

In the relationship, the distress could not stem from something itself. Yet ultimately, it will add to habits that create problems and anxiety for you and your spouse. Relationships may be one of the planet's most rewarding activities, but they can be a fertile ground for anxiety-related thoughts and emotions as well. At practically any point of courtship, relationship anxiety will occur. Only the idea of being in a relationship will create tension for several single individuals. If the early phases will provide us with constant worries as people start dating, all this anxiety about our relationships will make us feel pretty lonely. It can cause us to separate ourselves from our spouse. Our anxiety at its highest might also drive us to give up on love entirely. Learning more regarding the triggers and outcomes of anxiety in relationships will help us recognize the destructive feelings and behaviors that can sabotage our lives of love.

Causes or reasons for relationship anxiety:

Simply placed, getting in love surprises us in different forms that we do not predict. The more we trust somebody else, the further we stand to risk. We become afraid of getting injured on several occasions, both unconscious and conscious. To a considerable degree, we all share a distrust of intimacy. Unsurprisingly, this anxiety also occurs while we are having just what we expect, while we're feeling affection like we never had or being handled in ways which are unexpected. It's not about the stuff going on between our partner and us that makes us nervous when we get in a relationship; it is the stuff we say about what is going on to ourselves. The vital internal voice is a word used to characterize the mean coach in our heads who criticizes us, feeds us poor guidance, and fuels our own fear of being intimate. It is the one who says to us:

You are too fat/ugly/boring to hold his/her attention.

You cannot confide in him. He looking for some better person.

You are never going to encounter anyone, so why try even?

She does not love you for sure. Until you get hit, getaway.

This vital inner voice makes us and the other people close to us transform toward ourselves. It may facilitate aggressive, suspicious, and paranoid thought that decreases our self-esteem and pushes suspicion, defensiveness, envy, and anxiety to dangerous levels. Basically, rather than only loving it, it feeds us a steady stream of feelings that destroy our satisfaction and make us think about our relationship. We become extremely disconnected from the actual relationship with our partner while we get in our minds, dwelling on these worried feelings. We may tend to behave in negative ways, make nasty remarks, or become immature or parental towards our significant others. Imagine your partner remaining at work late one night, for instance. Sitting alone at home, the inner critic begins to remind you, 'Where is she?' Can you trust her for real? She wants to stay away from you, probably. She wants to stop you. She doesn't support you much either. Those feelings will accumulate in your head until you feel insecure, angry, or paranoid by the time your companion gets home. You can be upset or cold, which also makes your spouse feel angry and protective. Very fast, you changed the balance between you absolutely. You can spend a whole night feeling distant and angry with each other, instead of having a nice time you have together. Now you have essentially forced the difference you were originally afraid of. The reason behind this prophecy of self-fulfillment is not the condition itself. It's the vital inner voice that has colored your thought, skewed your perceptions, and eventually taken you down a damaging road.

Our own personal perceptions and modifications are the defenses we form and the vital voices we hear. Most of us have the capacity to get desperate and clingy in our acts when we feel stressed or nervous. In reaction, we may feel controlling or possessive towards our mate. Conversely, in our marriages, some of us can be quickly intruded on. We may withdraw from our spouses, distance ourselves from our desire. By being distant, aloof, or guarded, we can act out. These behavioral trends may emerge from our early forms of attachment. In our attachments in childhood, our attachment model is set and tends to serve as a functioning model for adult relationships. It affects how each one of us responds to our desires and how they are handled by us. Various attachment styles may cause one to feel various degrees of distress in relationships. You can read more about what the type of attachment is and how it influences the intimate partnerships here.

Thoughts that perpetuate anxiety in a relationship:

The unique vital inner voices that we have regarding ourselves, our spouses, and partnerships are developed by early attitudes to which we have been introduced in our families or in culture as a whole. Sexual assumptions as well as views about themselves & others that our powerful caretakers have had will invade our viewpoint and shadow our present perceptions. While the inner criticism of all is distinct, several typical inner critical voices include:

Critical inner voices that cause anxiety about the relationship:

Relationships will never work.

Individuals only end up being hurt.

Voices about your own self:

Do not be too fragile or you will just end up damaging yourself.

You would not ever meet another guy that knows you.

He does not worry for you that much.

Do not get stuck on her too soon.

On your own, you're better off.

You must hold him involved.

She would condemn you as soon as she gets to meet you.

When he is angry, it is your responsibility.

You must remain in charge.

Voices about one's partner:

He is cheating on you, probably.

Men are too selfish, insensitive, and unreliable.

He just worries about his buddies being around him.

Women are so needy, so fragile, and really indirect.

He cannot really do it right.

Why get enthusiastic like that? Anyway, what is so special about her?

You cannot confide in her.

Impacts of relationship anxiety:

We soon understand that there are many early forces that influenced our style of attachment, our mental defenses, and our vital inner voice as we shed light on our history. Both of these variables add to our relationship distress which may in several cases drive us to undermine our lives of marriage. The following behavior will result from listening to the inner critics and giving it into this anxiety:

Control: We can attempt to control or dominate our companion when we feel threatened. We should create guidelines for what they should and should not do only to ease our own feelings of fear or anxiety. Our companion may be offended by this action and generate frustration.

Cling: Our inclination might be to behave desperately towards our companion while we feel nervous. When we joined the relationship, we might quit acting like the powerful, strong individual we were. As a consequence, we can find ourselves quickly breaking apart, acting jealous or nervous, or no longer involved in individual activities.

Reject: One defense we may switch to is aloofness if we feel nervous about our relationship. To defend ourselves or beat our companion to the punch, we can be cold or deny. These actions can be overt or subtle, but our partner can often be a sure way of forcing distance or stirring up insecurity.

Punish: Our reaction to our fear is often more violent, and we simply punish, taking out our emotions on our mate. We can scream and shout, or we can send our companion a cold shoulder. It is important to pay our attention to how often our own actions respond to our companion and how much our inner voice responds to them.

Withhold: Often we prefer to withhold from our spouse while we feel nervous or scared, as opposed to direct rejection. Maybe things were moving close, and we felt worked up, so we withdrew. We hold back minor affections or give up completely on any part of our relationship. Withholding may seem a passive gesture, but in a partnership, it is one of the quietest killers of love and desire.

Retreat: In a relationship when we feel afraid, we can give up actual acts of love and affection and retreat into a fantasy bond. A fantasy relationship is a binding illusion that substitutes true actions of affection. We emphasis on shape over content in this state of imagination. In order to feel safe, we can stay in a relationship but give up on the important elements of the relationship. In a fantasy bond, as a way of creating distance and protecting ourselves against the discomfort that inevitably comes with having the freedom and in love, we sometimes participate in many of the negative behaviors listed above.

Overcoming relationship anxiety:

We ought to turn our attention inwards in order to alleviate relationship distress. Separate from our spouse or the relationship, we have to find out what is going on within us. What vital inner voices can our worries intensify? What defenses do we have that could build distance? This self-discovery phase may be a crucial step in recognizing and eventually influencing our interaction with the emotions that influence our behavior. We will obtain more understanding of where these emotions come from when digging into our history. What led us to feel uncomfortable in relation to marriage, or to turn on ourselves? By discovering all about fear of intimacy as well as how to recognize and resolve your vital inner voice, you will launch this process for yourself.

Detail of dealing with relationship anxiety:

Relationship anxiety relates to anxiety that exists in interpersonal relationships or anxiety based on relationships. It is not a known, diagnosable disorder and there are no recommendations on how to handle it as such, but it is an apparently common issue that is expected to impact around 1 in 5 persons. There are several explanations that anyone can feel nervous regarding their experiences. They may be fearful of being ignored or dismissed or fear that their sentiments are not rewarded. Some may fear that they will be unfaithful to their spouse or that the commitment won't last. Some may have reservations regarding being physically involved with a girlfriend or committing to some other person and losing out on other life choices.

Anxiety and its relationship with sex:

Anxiety can influence both a relationship's physical intimacy and sex life. For a variety of factors, fear may influence our libido or sexual desire, and it may even render sex difficulty, or impossible, on even a physical level. This may induce more distress and build a spiral that is negative. When feeling nervous, the troubling thoughts and stress we encounter will find it challenging to relax sufficiently to be able to fully enjoy sex or be conscious enough to be sexually involved with the other person. Sex-related worries, such as fears regarding performance, appearance, or being exposed to another human, may often find it extremely painful for certain individuals to have sex and interact physically, contributing to total rejection for others.

Anxiety and its relationship with dating:

Feelings of anxiety at the start of a relationship or even when dating are particularly common. Uncertainty about how the other person feels, or the status of your relationship, can be hard to tolerate before the relationship is properly established. To such a point that the resultant anxiety affects dating results, for example, feeling so conscious of yourself that it is impossible to establish eye contact or sustain a conversation, many individuals fear criticism or disapproval by others. In some individuals, this fear can be so great that they avoid dating altogether, despite desperately wanted to be in a relationship.

Reason for feeling anxious in relationships:

The tendency to feel insecure regarding relationships is also a product of the cycles of commitment that we encountered while we were young with our parents or caregivers. These affect how we recognize our needs and get them to be met. We are more likely to have a higher intensity of relationship anxiety if we have experienced anxiety attachment patterns. In a relationship, low self-esteem and a narrow outlook of yourself that is long-standing can also add to feelings of anxiety. If you believe you are not nice enough or might not have as much to give in a relationship as most people, so you are definitely going to assume that is what your spouse feels of you as well. The relation itself can cause you to feel anxious as well. If your spouse was secretive, critical, controlling, or violent, it would be normal to feel anxiety.

Signs and symptoms of relationship anxiety:

For most people, it is normal to experience several other levels of uneasiness or feel worried about the relationship at times, but this is more enduring and intense for others. Signs that you might be having relationship anxiety include the following:

- You also think about what you say to your wife, what your wife is like while you are not around and how your partnership is going to work out.
- You blow circumstances out of proportion, feeling hurt or angry at minor problems easily.
- When you think about your relationship, you feel regular signs of distress, such as sweatiness, tension, trouble concentrating.
- At the cost of your own needs, you go away from your own limits to please your partner.
- You also question your companion about their thoughts towards you for reassurance.
- When you are with your partner, you do not express your opinions or feelings and do not feel like you are willing to be yourself.
- With your partner, you are distant, aloof, or guarded, holding aspects of yourself away from them.
- You supply the companion with constructive comments or be demanding and commanding.
- You are clingy and want to be with your partner at all times.

- For example, by turning them away and see how much they are going to fight for you, you test the feeling of your partner for you.
- You are hesitant to be in a committed relationship or truly commit to your partner since you are terrified that it will not work out and that you'll be injured, upset, or deceived.
- In attempting to feel more in control, you destroy the relationship, such as meeting up with an 'ex' secretly.

Effects of relationship anxiety on you as well as on your relationship:

You might notice that your nervous feelings are getting more and more intense if your anxiety about relationships is not fixable. In the long run, this can trigger further hopelessness, anxiety, and depression. Relationship anxiety may also affect your partner and your relationship. It can lead in you trying to keep your partner at the length of your arms or even completely ending the relationship. By being controlling and confrontational or needy and passive, it also can be played out. Our acts influence how the other person feels and thereby react to us. Relationship anxiety can establish a prophecy that is self-fulfilling in certain situations, whereby the actions you exhibit as a consequence of your worries trigger the negative result that you feared. It might be necessary to do something about it if worry about your commitment becomes overwhelming, impacts your relationship, or impacts your quality of life.

How to overcome your relationship anxiety?

Some key strategies for getting over relationship anxiety are as follows:

Managing those things you usually do:

The things which we do also impacts the anxiety which we feel. You may be tempted to obtain reassurance or check in on your companion when you feel nervous. Although this can briefly make you feel happier, it will leave you feeling insecure in the long term and may even impact your relationship. Handling the stressful feelings that you have that cause your fear can contribute to long-lasting and meaningful improvement, thus minimizing acting out of distress. It can also help you to handle relationship anxiety and improve your relationship by communicating effectively with your partner, as it will give you both the chance to express how you experience and what you want and need from another person. It can be tempting to stop learning about tough challenges, but they normally do not seem to vanish and may generate anger.

Some individuals who experience anxiety in relationships can get caught in their anxiety-related thoughts that they forget other areas of life. Make sure you schedule time, every day, to do all the things you need to do to make yourself feel good. It can allow you to feel positive about yourself and to be more able to handle feelings of distress by continuing your own activities and interests, retaining many other relationships, and enjoying things that are essential to you.

Managing your way of thinking:

It is important to recognize your thoughts that are going to cause your anxiety. This could be detrimental feelings you have regarding yourself and your importance or a desire to interpret or draw conclusions about what others say about yourself or your mind. Make sure that the view you have is centered on the facts or reality of the condition rather than on the interpretations that you have made based on normal patterns of thinking and past experiences. Anxiety in relationships is always the product of constant fears. In responding to circumstances where the future is unpredictable, we appear to fear. The mind reflects on the possible bad consequences that might arise in order to offer us a sense of power. Practices in mindfulness will allow one to understand this habit of the mind. We will watch them come and go without giving up all efforts to brace for, or monitor, what occurs in the future by observing our thoughts and emotions with an attitude of interest and acceptance. This makes it possible for us to experience life without getting entangled in past pain stories, or imagined future concerns.

A brief CBT (Cognitive Behavior Therapy) course will help you boost your self-esteem, build a more balanced view of yourself, and understand how to more realistically perspective your relationship, which in turn can help you control how you feel.

Managing physical signs and symptoms of anxiety:

General methods in anxiety control will also make you feel more relaxed and confident, which can help you think more objectively and confidently in turn. It will all enable the mind and body to feel calmer if you take enough time off to rest and workout, have adequate sleep, practice yoga, listen to calming techniques or directed meditations, maintain a diary and eat regular, nutritious meals.

4.2 What is insecurity in relationships and how to recognize it?

We are just human, that also means that we all have our own personal insecurities of varying intensities, even the most self-confident folks among us. It can be hard to identify and recognize these insecurities, let alone work through them, but if you want to live a good, happy life, it is crucial to figure out how to control your insecurities. Those insecurities will have a significant effect on too many aspects of your life, like your love life, if left unchecked. That is why it is so important to know how your self-doubt affects a commitment and recognize the signs that yours is causing trouble in your love life.

In an intimate relationship, have you ever faced uncertainty and wondered whether it implied it your beloved other was not the best individual for you? Those with an attachment style that is secure usually have fewer problems, are often happy, and are commonly better at helping their partner, so this raises the question that you can start teaching yourself to stop your relationship from being insecure, and if so, how? First of all, vulnerability is much deeper than confidence, because it drives a loss of emotional trust and stability. You seem to have all trust in the universe that you would not be cheated on by your mate, but you also feel vulnerable. And while an increase in the use of technology can cause jealousy and influence how safe we feel with our companion. In fact, our core insecurities often emerge from attachment scars, which is a way of describing a significant relationship at any time that has broken our confidence in the past. This will produce defensiveness that drives people out and robs us of the chance to actually allow others in.

This is where in a relationship of yours, becoming nervous and questioning whether you are with the right guy fits in, you can be nervous in the relationship and be with the correct guy completely. You may be just self-destroying because you are scared to let someone in too closely, because when this tends to happen, it may be because you are not aware of your style or attachment, assumptions, projections, insecurities, and behaviors (or just do not know how to handle them). If you feel that you are unhealthy, then collaborate through counseling and self-awareness to decide if it stems from other sources or whether you are simply in an unpleasant relationship.

Signs and Symptoms of insecurities causing hurdles in relationship:

It is when things always begin to fall down as ideas become motion. It is normal to feel very nervous or a little paranoid/jealous. We may be quite possessive, without even realizing it at times. You can think about all sorts of things, and your choices do not really direct you. When you begin to act on your insecurities, however, this changes. You could become too dependent on your companion if insecurities of yours are not kept in check. Clearly define, if your self-doubt insecurities cause you to feel negative emotions that later display into negative behaviors that is when some of the adverse effects of the insecurity can start to feel in your relationship. It may not change quickly, but know that if you want to work through certain insecurities, even if that is alone, with your therapist, or even with your partner's love and support, it's okay. Here are several important indicators that, according to psychologists, your insecurities or self-doubt are having an effect on your relationship.

Internalizing your pessimistic thoughts and convert them into healthy actions:

From time to time, it is normal to have negative feelings or thoughts, but if you bring yourself down often, you will ultimately internalize certain negative feelings, and those manipulative thoughts will also alter how you behave, which is likely to influence your relationship. If you repeat things many times and carry it out as a person continuously, due to your acts, your relationship will shift. For starters, if you keep doing things which make you sound weak and sad, you will gradually start feeling exactly that. In turn, this will spill into your relationship and have a major effect on the mate. It is not because you are not permitted to judge on your own. Do so, but try to be a wise counselor when you do so, not a vicious dictator.

Trusting in your partner can be difficult:

You question all, you snoop on your wife, you stalk social networking pages, or you feel quickly challenged are the indicators of faith that your wife is giving you a very rough time.

Step to take: Practice meditation and journaling while you feel like this. See where you should question your thoughts to look for a situation and extend the benefit of the doubt to your mate.

Why: It makes you question the habits of pessimistic thinking and lets you become more mindful of where the emotions come from. Instead of projecting them into your mate and then hyper-focused on the possibly meaningless and irrelevant, you can understand how to properly deal with emotions and feelings.

Reading too keenly into your partner's sayings:

Under any particular circumstance, if you always find yourself guessing what your spouse thinks about you, and you often believe the worst, it is a strong indication that your negative thoughts and feelings are messing with your relationship. You continue to read through your partner's comments in a way that confirms the insecurities that you have. You may consider them to be disloyal or not to you, and the relationship focuses on showing the emotions that the individual has instead of enjoying the time.

Struggling with the factor of intimacy:

You struggle to feel emotionally or sexually connected to each other or both. During intimate times, you can sense your guard up. There are all the indicators of your relationship showing you that you're dealing with intimacy.

Action to take: Intimacy as well as what it represents to you and the partner must first be recognized. Question yourself if closeness and affection are perceived the same way by you and the partner. Then focus on where the guards are from, the expectations of society, insecurity, past abuse, fears.

Why: It can help you connect with your companion so that both of you will be on the same level. For each other, be polite and understand the disagreements.

Trouble in trusting your partner:

Having shared trust is important if you want a stable partnership. If your insecurities keep you from trusting and respecting your partner entirely, it makes it hard for you to start opening emotionally, also, which could really stunt the development of your partnership. You are reluctant to put confidence and faith in others, and this could harm the partnership because you cannot or would not open up and it sets a cap on the amount of personal contact that you are about to share.

Being panicked easily:

You fear that your spouse may oppose you during a fight, withdraw, or may judge that you will trigger fear in you.

Step to take: Recognize this feeling of fear the very first time you experienced it and point it to an incident to see if it plays a part in the present circumstance. So what would you need to know, and now what do you need to know? If it is the same, as you begin to feel activated again, consider reminding yourself the message.

Why: It offers you the freedom to feel as you feel, which is validating and relaxing indeed. It also provides you insight into previous patterns and factors that can assist you to view situations from a certain viewpoint so that you can soften the panic and engage more rationally.

Comparing yourself to the exes of your partner:

Until you come along, it is just normal to be concerned about who your mate was with, so if you're always contrasting yourself to the exes of your partner and worried that you do not match up, it is a sure indication that your relationship is influenced by your insecurities. If your lover is into you, and you keep on having a contrast, you might be ruined. All the detrimental what-ifs are possible killers in relationships. If you have strong contact with your girlfriend, so this is an uncertainty that can be suppressed with the expression 'Who are they really with now? Me, or an ex of theirs? '. Let that be who you would be, for you and for the partner, whether you are trying to equate yourself to someone.

Feeling being attacked easily:

You feel insulted, annoyed, or shut down instantly by what your spouse demands of you. You feel criticized quickly and try to protect yourself by debating or completely shutting down are all symptoms and indications you will instantly feel assaulted.

Measure to take: ask the following questions:

Really, what did my wife/husband say?

How much of my theories are hypotheses?

Will there be a risk that I can internalize this condition and make it something it is not?

The way: It makes you question your perceptions and look through an analytical perspective at the situation. Without hyper-emotion, you can recognize what your companion is attempting to interact with.

Depending on your partner to make you feel as you actually exist:

Self-acceptance is not something that can be summoned immediately, so if you focus entirely on your spouse to make you feel appropriate, desirable enough, fun enough, wise enough, kind enough, you are never going to be truly satisfied, both in you and in your relationship. You name it, an anxious person would worry whether any given standard is ever appropriate for them. Yet there is the tyranny of what is enough. You do not feel appropriate, and you look to your companion to redefine something for you because you are searching for something which comes from inside all the time: radical recognition of yourself.

You take little things as complex issues:

Until you have taken a step back, you use definitive or hurtful terms, chose battles to render them extreme problems, to build massive arguments over something that is not really large are all the indications that you take little items as complicated issues.

Action to take: Focus on three to five fights you have seen in the past and look critically at them. Tell yourself what was behind the stuff in which you were complaining and attempt to define trends.

The reason: You will be able to detect internal trends that you were not conscious of. Maybe you are creating larger points out of tiny information because you never thought a huge concern was absolutely fixed; maybe you are trying to make yourself feel very connected to somebody because you are sabotaging joy; maybe you have desires that are not fulfilled in your relationship, but it's simpler to struggle over the laundry or who they posted to Instagram instead of discussing them directly.

You want your partner for defining your validity:

Every once in a while, there is nothing unusual with wanting some reassurance from your mate, but if you need them continuously to affirm you, it is an indication that your negative thoughts and feelings are getting the best of you, and if they get bored of convincing you, that might make you even more anxious. The drifting patience of your companion to comfort you can imply that you are relying too hard on your partner and doing nothing for yourself. This may be the mark of a serious, unsupportive spouse that is potentially adding to your vulnerability as your spouse lacks patience for your desire for reassurance.

You are not accepting yourself:

When it comes to granting yourself permission to only be you,

you always criticize yourself and keep yourself to high expectations, all the indications that you face trouble embracing yourself are failing.

Action to take: Focus on yourself so that you do not slip into a co-dependency trap and cannot allow your true self to evolve. Go to therapy, read journals, bring the soulful or spiritual efforts into motion. Look at the effect of your experience on your present, and grant permission to yourself to move through it. Offer yourself, most especially, grace and love.

The reason: To soothe or fix your perceived difficulties, you learn not to depend on others in an unfair way. You are going to get the personal trust and empowerment to authentically show up. It also lets you recognize causes and subconscious forces such that in the future you can restore, soothe, or prevent them.

Distance in relationship:

One of the greatest aspects of a relationship is experiencing your partner's intimate relational closeness. But it can really have a negative impact on your relationship if your insecurities lead you to keep your spouse at a distance. Your insecurities render you both feel disconnected from each other, or you have trouble connecting and sharing your doubt and insecurities, and it is translated in some apparent forms that you are bothered by something. Your companion may pick up on energies or facial movements or actually sense like there is something that they cannot repair inside of you.

Managing your insecurities in your relationship:

In the end, it is necessary to note that everybody has insecurities, so it is almost difficult to stop getting instances of insecurity in the relationship. How a person manages or does not manage, their personal insecurities is what really breaks or makes a relationship. Some insecurities, especially if you're in a relationship for the first time, are natural and safe. With every new experience, that comes. It is important to have faith and integrity in the opportunity to be open about your issues with your partner. If there is an inappropriate and unnecessary degree of insecurity, therefore it might be necessary to obtain outside support from a therapist that may help further explain what is occurring at a therapeutic level. It is completely up to you to take the time to focus on your relation with yourself if you'd like to learn to control your doubt and insecurities and lessen their influence on your intimate relationships, how you continue your path to acceptance, and self-love.

How to overcome insecurities in your relationship?

The next thing you can do is interact with your spouse efficiently. Why does your spouse interact? What is their form of communication? You might repeatedly chat about stuff, but until you actually talk with your companion at their stage, addressing lingering concerns can be difficult. The great news is, you will collaborate to resolve romantic insecurities with your mate. It can require patience, efficient contact, and the ability to deepen the relationship, however, it can be accomplished. Here are some of the most successful ways to avoid feeling unsafe:

You should stop psyching out yourself:

Your emotions may be the best buddy or worst enemy in your relationship. The consistency of your thoughts influences the quality of the relationship directly. Have you ever noticed thinking pessimistic thoughts like, one day you know they are going to get sick of you or, how do they accept you? These theories have nothing to do with reality, but they have a great deal to do with anxiety. In other words, this is not a dilemma you're obsessed about, you invented it. Whenever you feel uncertain about the relationship, remind yourself that the issue you are concerned about happens just in your mind. You have got total control.

Understanding the needs of each other:

Every single individual in the world has six fundamental human needs which concern them. We always aspire to be sure that we can escape pain and happiness, that we want to feel important, that we want diversity in life, that interaction with others is necessary, and that development and commitment allow us to find fulfillment. These needs are categorized in a different manner by each person, so consider the one that is most essential to your partner. Will the relationship allow their desires to be fulfilled? If not, how do you adjust your habits so that you feel more valued and accepted by your partner? You must consider and decide on your own.

Stop relating all to yourself:

You are going to get a worldview self-centered pursuing boogeymen in which they do not live. Do not say it is because of you if your companion doesn't feel like heading out when they might have had a very rough day at work that wasted their energy almost as quickly. In order to notice the meaning behind their speech, body appearance, and stance, avoid psycho-analyzing any choice of words your spouse uses to be more present at the moment. A sure work way to skip the argument is to obsess over concealed definitions. Do not ridicule your companion for being too silent, or inquire constantly, what do you think? During a conversation lapse, the pattern of an anxious person is an intense desire to fill any second of quiet with needless phrases. Take the side of your spouse, breathe out, breathe in, and together, embrace the quiet. Who says you cannot love just living without words with each other? Definitely, you can.

Balancing your directions or polarity:

There is one spouse with male energy in any relationship and the other with female energy. These forces or energies do not have to match with sex, but in an attempt to find romantic equilibrium, opposing powers need to be involved. This concept is known as polarity. Have you developed an unbalanced or inconsistent relationship with your partner? It may trigger insecurities to emerge if all spouses carry on male or female characteristics. Look at how the functions have evolved over time and how polarity can be preserved and fear can be banished.

Stop overloading yourself:

Have you ever felt so bad in a relationship that you would love

to only wish that it is all away so that you never have to hear about it again? Only enter a club. Since this love type of thing is an unexpected and often rough journey, you will be pressed hard to find a guy who does not have a bit of baggage. A little baggage or junk is totally fine, but before jumping into any new relationship, you need to loosen your load. Let go of any hurtful feelings leftover that might linger and realize that the new relationship is a fresh chance to put all that behind you. The beautiful thing about this life is that you can start again many times as you will need to.

Feel like you are just a new couple:

The energy is thrilling when you started to date someone new. Whenever necessary, you want to discover more about your companion and be emotionally near to them. This spark disappears with time. The sparks you first experienced started to fizzle as you get more acquainted with your mate. In your routines, you get relaxed and quit striving to please. When your partner thinks like you are no longer making an attempt or that the attraction of yours is decreasing, insecurities will emerge. In your relationship, put back the spark and behave as you did before you were dating. Give compliments to your partner. Plan unexpected dates. Write love notes to them. These little gestures will help to reduce insecurities and aid to feel wanted

by your partner.

Stop feeling suffocating over nothing:

Since we all refer to individuals of the same sex, let us face it. Just because they are buddies with a boy and a girl doesn't imply there is more to the tale. Stop the urge to snoop on the Facebook posts, computer, or email address of your partner. While this could momentarily relax your anxiety when you do not see anything afoul, it is still a habit that could become addictive easily, not to mention harmful for relationship confidence when they figure out that big brother is observing.

Stop seeing dark in things:

If anyone accuses you of anything which you do not believe is your responsibility, how do you react? You will become defensive. Similarly, questioning your companion about an issue would most definitely lead them to become aggressive, no matter how clear it might be to you. This generally leads to a drag-out, knock-down fight that is the reverse of positive when all of you are too busy attempting to show that you are correct to settle your disagreement. Do not point the finger instantly if you have a dilemma, but instead treat your companion with sensitivity and empathy. Be secure of the reality that none of you is completely right or wrong. Somewhere in the center lies the real answer.

To create some healthy stories:

Even in all the best relationships, errors are made, however, steady relationships will leave such mistakes in the past. What are you living with, you or your partner? No matter whether you have already struggled for money or flirtations, it is time to put those old stories behind if you are deciding to move on as a couple. Try changing your attitude instead of believing that your companion is constantly doing something that bothers you. Respect your mate for who they are, and instead of replaying past trauma, plan to build a wonderful new tale together. Insecurities in all the most successful relationships are likely to emerge from time to time. You cannot monitor the feelings of your mate, but you can become the most compassionate, caring version possible of yourself.

Stop being over-dependent on others:

Nothing small of wonderful is finding someone to make love to, cuddle, hug, kiss, and live your own life with. But you need to first learn to respect yourself before you march out into the sunset in pursuit of love. You should not welcome a companion into your life when it is in disarray, just as you should not welcome a guest to your house while it is a disorganized mess. Take caution before welcoming someone else to your inner-house. You should predict the side effects of decreased stress

and improved partner fulfillment if you let your insecurities go.

Learn to face uncomfortable conversations:

While the conflict in the short term is painful for the relationship, it will strengthen the intensity of your relation in the long term. Without a doubt, confronting your concerns will make you develop closer to your spouse. Never grind words with another and you can build confidence so deep that you can say your partner everything that has been on your mind.

4.3 What is jealousy in relationships and how to build trust in the couple?

No one likes to feel jealous. Yet, jealousy is an unavoidable feeling that would be witnessed by nearly anyone of us. The concern with jealousy is not when it pops about from time - to

- time, but when we do not have a grip on it, what it does to us. Experiencing what occurs when we enable our jealousy to overtake us or form the way we feel regarding ourselves and the environment around us may be terrifying. That is why knowing where our jealous emotions really come from and discovering how to cope with jealousy in positive, adaptive ways are vital to our personal ambitions in so many aspects of our lives, from our personal relations to our jobs.

Why we get jealous?

Studies have shown, predictably, that enhanced jealousy coincides with low self-esteem. Most of us are also ignorant of the simple guilt that resides inside us, so it comes too easily to have self-critical feelings about ourselves. Yet, guilt from our experience will strongly affect the extent to which we feel uncomfortable and jealous of the present. A mode of negative self-talk is a vital inner speech. With great scrutiny, it perpetuates negative thoughts and emotions, driving us to equate, assess, and analyze ourselves (and sometimes others). This is one explanation of why it is so necessary to learn how to cope with jealousy. By loading our minds with critical and suspect commentary, this voice will fuel our jealousy feeling. Really, it is always difficult to deal with what our sensitive inner voice advises us regarding our condition than the condition itself. Our partner's rejection or betrayal is traumatic, but what sometimes scares us even worse is all the awful thoughts that our inner voice informs us about us after the incident. You are a fool. Have you really felt that you should never be happy? Alone, you will end up. Never again do you believe anyone. We will look more closely at two forms of jealousy to explain how this internal adversary feeds our negative emotions about jealousy: romantic jealousy and competitive jealousy. Although these two types of jealousy sometimes intersect, we can better grasp how jealous emotions can impact various aspects of our lives & how we might best cope with jealousy by understanding them separately.

Competitive jealousy:

Although it can sound illogical or pointless, having what everyone else has and feeling jealous is totally normal. How we use these impulses, though, is quite key to our degree of fulfillment and enjoyment. That is simply a negative trend of demoralizing consequences if we use these emotions to satisfy our inner opponents, to bring down us or others. If we don't let these emotions fall into our vital inner voice's lap, though, we will potentially leverage them to understand what we desire, to be more goal-oriented, or simply to be more tolerant with ourselves and what influences us. It's all right, even safe, to encourage ourselves to think in a competitive way. When we actually let us have a temporary sensation without judgment or a timetable for action, it may feel pleasant. However, we end up getting hurt if we ruminate or distort this idea into a critique of ourselves or an assault on another human. We will do many things if we find ourselves feeling haunted or getting an overreaction by our feelings of jealousy.

Be conscious of what gets allowed. Think of the particular occurrences that lead you to feel excited. Is it a buddy who is financially successful? A co-worker who in meetings expresses her mind? An ex who dates someone else?

Think of these thoughts' broader meanings and origins: Do you sense a certain urge to accomplish a certain thing? What does it entail to make this thing for you? Is there someone else you believe you are going to be? Will the past contribute to this?

Tell yourself what inner vital voices are increasing. What kind of ideas are triggered by these jealous feelings? Do they render you feel negligible, incompetent, inefficient, etc.? Do you put yourself down by using these emotions of jealousy? Is there a trend or motif which sounds familiar to these thoughts?

When we have asked ourselves such questions, we will appreciate how these emotions could have much to do with unsolved problems within ourselves than with our present life or with the entity to whom our jealousy is guided. We should have more self-pity and strive to remove the assumptions that cause us to feel uncomfortable.

Romantic jealousy:

It is a simple fact that when people do not get too jealous, relationships go better. The sooner we grab control of our emotions of jealousy & make logical sense of them apart from our mate, the happier we're going to be. Note, our jealousy also stems through our own fear, a sense of being cursed to be betrayed, ignored, or harmed. Until we cope with this feeling inside ourselves, in every relationship, regardless of the circumstances, we are prone to drop prey to feelings of mistrust, jealousy, or fear. These pessimistic thoughts towards ourselves originate in our life from very early encounters. We also carry in emotions that our parents or major caretakers either had towards us or towards themselves. We then, in our present relationships, repeat, unintentionally, replicate, or react to familiar, old dynamics. For starters, if we felt set out as children, our spouse might possibly be viewed as ignoring us. We could prefer a more elusive partner or even indulge in activities that might drive our partner away.

In our adult lives, particularly in relationships of ourselves, the level to which we have taken on self-critical behaviors as children also shapes how often our inner critical voice can impact us. And, no matter whatever our particular perspectives might be, to a degree we all share this inner critic. Most of us will contribute to a sense that we will not be preferred to bring around. The level to which we assume this anxiety determines how threatened in a relationship we can feel.

Negative thoughts towards ourselves are always hidden behind the hostility towards our friends or the critiques towards a supposed third-party risk. Thoughts such as, what is he seeing in her? She will easily become so much thinner / prettier / more powerful than you. And when our worst thoughts materialize and we hear about the affair of a parent, we always react by aiming anger at us because we are dumb, destroyed, unwanted or unlovable. Our vital inner voice advises us, like a sadistic teacher, not to believe or be too weak. It reminds us that we are not lovable and not romantically cut out. The soft whisper is what implants a seed of uncertainty, fear, and distrust. Why does she work late? Why would he have to pick his buddies over me? How is it that he gives too much importance to what she says? These are all the concerns concerning your spouse that might render you doubtful.

Many of us experienced with how the feeling of jealousy operates realize that these feelings will eventually begin to sprout and grow into even bigger, more embedded assaults on us and our partner, all too frequently. She has no reason to hang with you. Will anyone else has to be present, who will like to listen and talk to you? You are so boring, he loses interest in you. He needs you to getaway. At every stage in a relation, from the first meeting to the twentieth year of the marriage, this jealous feeling will emerge. We may respond to the inner critics and step away from being near to our partner in an effort to defend ourselves. Yet, in the perfect catch 22, after we have withdrawn from doing what we desire, we still seem to get more jealous. We seem to become more vulnerable and much more jealous of whether we realize at any stage that we are not keeping our relation a focus or consciously moving for our objective of being close or loving. It is why knowing how to cope with jealousy is much more important and not blindly acting on insecure emotions or pushing our spouse farther apart.

Major signs and symptoms telling that your partner is getting jealous:

It might not be something you realize at first to deal with a jealous spouse because, odds are, it's veiled as being something fresher to begin. And while it does not sound like a big deal if your wife has jealous behaviors, jealousy lists domestic abuse as a warning sign. Although it doesn't imply that any jealous entity can become violent, it does imply that in a relationship, jealousy is an addictive characteristic and something you can keep a close eye on. If you have a suspicion that you might be interacting with such a jealous spouse, but are not yet positive if their acts suit the bill, you can watch out for any big subtle indicators.

If you want to spend with your own self that will be an issue for them:

You need to be in a position to do some of your own things. It may seem that separation from your partner, even for just a second, can also be impossible if you are used to spending most or all of the time with your spouse. However, it does not imply it is difficult or not quite fun. It is certainly a form of jealousy if your companion makes a huge deal while you want to do your things. For partners to spend some time alone and have different hobbies is common. If your spouse disagrees with your private time from her or him, it may suggest jealousy, regardless of the explanation given. He or she may be scared that while you're gone, you'll find someone else.

Checking up on you every time:

They need to give you room. It is good to submit or receive a nice text wondering about their day is going while you are not having time together with your partner, right? But if such texts are getting received all the time all day, then you'll need to be concerned. If you are just worried about your relationship when you are with other people, it may be a result of jealousy instead of sincere concern. This could include checking in on you while you are out with buddies or at a job event, typically in the interest of making sure you are all right, by texts and calls.

Questioning every friendship of you:

Keep on the alert for this red flag. Relationships can be formed from honesty, and you should consider it as a warning flag of jealousy if your spouse has trouble with the friends you have. Jealous people are also worried that you choose one of your mates to date, so they try to restrict your friendship group. It could mean jealousy if your spouse continues to bully you into avoiding friends or ask to clean up your social network followers.

Even mentioning someone else will be a problem for them:

It might sound small, but it's a huge deal. Jealous mates often have trouble discussing somebody else from your background or even in the present life, particularly if it is somebody they think you may be a little drawn to. If you discuss a passing friend, and they get nervous instantly, this is a warning. They might make any sarcastic remark or just seem clearly in a dark mood, but you may get a clear feeling that they did not appreciate the way that anyone else was listed. As a slight backhanded remark, these jealous attitudes may start out, but with time they will intensify.

Stalking your social media:

Your social network should not have your wife criticized. Nowadays, before they transform into real-life encounters, several relationships originate on social media, so it is not out of the norm to see anyone like many photos of yours to gain your attention. If you are in a relationship and something occurs or anything you share is up for dispute, so you might be living with a jealous girlfriend. They are first to like it if you share a selfie. If you check-in at bar A when you inform them you are moving to bar B, before you can set your mobile phone down, you will get a text or email about it. They liked the images you shared about a year ago on Instagram. These are all warning signs that you are being watched too closely by this person. Another illustration may be a random reference to the time you moved to Thailand a couple of years back, but you never said that to them. If anyone has stalked your social networking accounts, they might give away them by only knowing about you a little too much.

Accusing you of cheating every time, even if they pretend to joke:

This is not a joke. Actually, finding a companion with whom you can chat and smile over something is a God send. However, when your unfaithfulness, whether theoretical or actual, becomes the focus of jokes all of the time, you definitely contend with a jealous girlfriend. Would your wife ever suspect you, even as a joke, of cheating? A jealous spouse may place their remarks as humor in the initial stages of the relationship, however, they return a lot to the topic. When you spend some time on your mobile phone or request to see the text messages, do they get nervous? Both these are powerful indicators of someone possessing a jealous attitude.

They always try to have control over your behavior:

A spouse in charge is no good. It is really common in relationships to establish expectations for your partner on what you do not want and what you do. When your companion tries his or her utmost to convince you of what you have to do and how you have done it, it becomes a challenge. This is manipulative and a symptom of jealousy if your companion wants you to do something like praising them all the time. Such stuff, such as not contradicting with them in front of anyone or asking you to pay heed to them, is stuff that you can still be careful about.

They will start a fight with you every time when you are going out somewhere:

They do not want to go out with you. When you spend time apart from your spouse, checking up on you while you are out or sitting silently with a mood are also indicators of jealousy, but beginning a big war when you quit is often a warning you can pay attention to. When you are going to head out or at a function, whether they pick petty arguments with you, it is because you do not go out or quit so that you will quit the event early. The purpose of this activity is to restrict and prohibit the other participant from communicating or socializing with anyone else from getting some chance. The aim is to separate the partner or cause them pain so that they do not feel comfortable heading out or sitting at the case.

They want details of everything from you:

A feeling of freedom should be felt by you. It is far from safe to be handled as if you are a kid in a relationship and it is a telltale indication that you are coping with a jealous spouse. They want you to have a comprehensive account to cover in the holes if your companion is unable to check for your locations. This is achieved in order to track who and what you are around or what you're doing. A jealous spouse is searching for a theme to define and decide if you spend so much time with a single person.

They are so concerned to win you over:

Sweet movements have secret intentions often. You will find that if you are with a jealous spouse, they will go out of their own way to do something that would make you express love. At first, it may seem good, but you will note after a while that something just is not quite right. They would try anything in their capacity to make you love them if your spouse is jealous. To make you feel like if you ought to convince them that you just have eyes for themselves and they have zero reasons to be concerned, they can do anything imaginable.

They act as if they have no care:

That is counter-intuitive, but they do care about it. Partners prefer to participate in conversations along with others in most stable relationships. The goal is to function together to demonstrate unison, whether one partner understands the additional individuals in a discussion better than their spouse or not. However, if your mate tries to leave you dangling at all times, you would definitely be living with a jealous mate. When you speak to other individuals and pretend like they cannot care less, if your beloved appears to neglect you, it means they cannot care more. In social environments, pay heed to how they behave with you.

How to overcome jealousy in a relationship?

One of the greatest joys of life is good romantic relationships, incorporating companionship, fun, and love into the lives of both spouses. It acts as an anchor, lifeboat, and sail that holds you afloat, comfortable, and filled with intent while your relationship is built on confidence. The bond becomes a burden that hinders professional development as jealousy erodes the trust and esteem of your partnership. For a stable marriage, learning how to avoid being insecure in a relationship is a requirement. You should focus on yourself to overcome jealousy and build a meaningful relationship, no matter what burden the other individual brings to the game.

How to overcome jealousy in a relationship?

How would jealousy have an impact on intimate relations? It works against the three components of love, the universal ideals of forming a healthy, trusting union. It becomes difficult to uphold the discipline of genuine love and kindness because jealousy impairs the capacity to love without obstacles. When jealousy is a concern, it is often difficult to be completely insecure, because jealousy causes tension in your relationship. Envy covers discernment and, through simple suspicions, it becomes difficult to tell the facts. When you are insecure, you cannot allow your companion the freedom to live a life, nor can you ever be able to live a life of your own when coping with an insecure companion. Jealousy can move into all facets of your life, finding it impossible to appreciate anything. When the feeling of jealousy in a relationship is given complete sway, no party thrives. When you let envy go unregulated, your relationship will suffer. It involves being truthful with your partner and with your own self to realize how to avoid being a competitive boyfriend or girlfriend. Get to the root of your envy and create the dynamic of a healthy partnership.

4.4 How to eliminate negative thinking and fear of abandonment?

In social and success scenarios, negative thought leads to anxiety. Many social anxiety treatments have an element devoted to transforming harmful modes of thought into more helpful more optimistic forms of thinking of scenarios. The trick to overcoming your negative thinking is to consider how you feel now (and the concerns that result) and to use techniques to alter thinking or allow them to have less effect. These measures are typically worked out through a doctor, although they may often be done to resolve social distress as one of a self-help initiative.

Effective strategies to change negative thinking:

Such essential and most powerful tips for transforming destructive behaviors and turning these negative emotions into optimistic thoughts are as follows:

Avoid stopping your thoughts:

If you have anxiety issues, don't try and control one's negative feelings. It would just cause social distress worse and attempt to escape suicidal feelings. Stopping thoughts is the contrary of meditation. It is the process of being on the lookout for new for and insisting that negative thoughts be eliminated. The trouble with stopping thoughts is that the more pessimistic thoughts you want to avoid, the more they can emerge. Meditation is preferable as it gives your thoughts less weight and decreases the impact they see on oneself. Stopping thinking would seem to aid in the brief period, but it leads to even more anxiety over time.

Understanding your own thinking patterns:

To reduce social anxiety, stop thinking in real terms. Healthy and dark thinking can trigger anxiety in society. Understanding exactly how those who feel right now is one of the first stages towards changing your negative thoughts. For instance, if you continue to view yourself in every situation as a total success or failure, then you engage in healthy and dark thinking. Some patterns in pessimistic thought include leaping to catastrophizing, assumptions, and over dramatization. Patterns of unhelpful thinking differ in complex ways. But they all constitute reality distortions and inappropriate ways of thinking about situations and individuals.

How to face criticism positively?

Socially insecure adults continue to focus on the skills of assertiveness. If you do have social anxiety, you will train to protect yourself. In addition to cognitive improvement, something recognized as the assertive protection of the self includes another component of CBT that is also useful. As it is likely that people would genuinely be negative and judgmental against you some of the time, it is crucial that you can cope with disapproval and criticism. This approach is typically carried out in counseling to develop up your assertiveness abilities and assertive reactions to feedback through a pretend dialogue between you and your psychiatrist. By homework tasks, these talents are then applied to the physical world.

Learn to stop your negative thinking patterns:

To fight social anxiety, change your negative thoughts. CBT for social anxiety could even help to turn around negative thoughts. Cognitive restructuring is one of the basic elements of a treatment regimen that included cognitive-behavioral therapy (CBT). This method helps you to identify negative thoughts into more useful and adaptive responses and change them. Cognitive restructuring, whether done in medication or on your own, includes a step-by-step process by which negative thoughts are identified, assessed for consistency, and then replaced. Even if it is challenging to think at first in this modern form, constructive and logical thoughts can emerge more easily over time and with practice.

Learn to have mindfulness in your conscious:

To decrease social anxiety, use mindfulness. Mindfulness can help reduce anxiety in society. Mindfulness in meditation has its roots. It is the practice of detaching yourself and observing them as an outside observer from your thoughts and emotions. You will understand how to view your feelings and thoughts as objects flying past you during mindfulness training, which you can stop and observe or let cross you by. The goal of meditation is to take control of your emotional responses to circumstances by allowing your brain's thinking part to take over.

Keeping your diary for thought collection:

To record the social tension on a regular basis, use a thinking diary. To capture your everyday feelings on social anxiety, a thought journal may be used. In order to modify critical thoughts, mind diaries, also called mind archives, may be used as part of any method. Think diaries allow you to recognize types of unpleasant thinking and to gain insight into how your emotional responses are triggered by your emotions (and not the circumstances you are in). As part of regular assignments, most CBT diagnostic tests will entail the use of a thinking diary. A thought journal entry, for example, could break down a person's thinking process on a date, and the physical and emotional responses that arise from negative patterns of thinking. You should swap emotional feelings regarding rejection for more helpful and optimistic forms of thinking of the conclusion of the thought study.

If you are dealing with unhealthy ways of thinking and your life is impaired, try speaking to a mental health specialist. While expressing the feelings you have with others can be challenging, therapists can analyze the destructive ways of thinking to help you build a positive inner dialogue.

Strategies to eliminate the fear of abandonment in a healthy way:

Each of us has fears of becoming left alone. Many of us are struggling with some basic emotions which we are unlovable or will not be embraced for who we really are. We all have a cynical inner ear, an internal pessimistic debate that criticizes us chronically or offers us poor advice. Our fear of abandonment is often perpetuated by this voice. He's about to abandon you, you're warned. She's probably cheating, she's even making you cry. Since we both have voices and warnings that are set off as we feel triggered, getting instruments and techniques to settle down as we notice our concerns being heightened is useful. One helpful guide is this toolkit for helping people live with fear, which outlines workouts that are helpful while they get worked up for us to use. Another general practice to be adopted is that of compassion for oneself. It has countless advantages. In fact, trying to improve self-compassion is beneficial to establish self-confidence, because benevolence doesn't quite concentrate so much on judgment and assessment. Instead, it contains three key elements:

The technique of mindfulness:

Being mindful is necessary because it helps individuals just don't over-identify in order to allow them to get swept away with their feelings and thoughts. If people are terrified of things like being lost, they prefer to reinforce this anxiety with a lot of mean thinking about themselves. Imagine that, without having them overwhelm you, you might remember these thoughts and emotions. Could you take a kinder attitude towards yourself, and instead of flying off with them, have those thoughts pass like dark clouds without losing one's sense of yourself.

The technique of showing kindness to yourself:

It comes from the idea that individuals should be kind to themselves, as contrasted to judgmental. In theory, this sounds simple, but in practice, it is much more challenging. In the face of challenging conditions, the more individuals can have a warm, embracing attitude towards themselves and their hardships, the stronger they will feel. Even if we feel upset or dumped by someone else, we can all be better friends with ourselves.

Common acceptance of humanity:

And each of us can admit that we are human and we will even struggle in our lives, like all humans, the more we can cultivate self-compassion and stability. When people are able to realize constantly that they are not lonely and that they are deserving, they can encourage themselves to stop accepting such negative and wrong tweets, informing them that they are going to be abandoned or discarded.

Overcoming your fear of abandonment:

Fear of abandonment can be very true and very traumatic, but when people can exercise self-compassion, when they're activated, they're more able to get through those moments. The more people can trace these emotions to one's roots in with their past, the more these experiences can be separated from the present. It requires bravery for anyone to be able to see what hurt themselves and to confront the main feelings of loss they might have experienced because they had little power over their condition as children. However, they can set oneself free from some of the other chains of their past when people are willing to face these feelings. They will become distinguished adults who can build new stories and new partnerships where only they feel heard, protected, comforted, and therefore absolutely healthy.

4.5 How to resolve conflicts and save your relationship?

As someone who's been in an intimate companionship

understands, there are frequent conflicts and battles. If two people, in their life, entangled, spend too much time with one another, they are expected to vary even from occasionally. Such discrepancies may be broad or minor, varying from whether to prepare for supper or refusing to accomplish a mission to conflicts on whether the pair can switch to the profession of one person or compromise on the religious education of children. The very fact you're arguing with your wife isn't an indication that your friendship is in serious danger. In reality, combat will deepen your partnership when done properly. You would never fix them unless you never battle and never speak about your issues. You will achieve a greater view of your companion and come to a compromise that fits for all of you when coping with disputes productively. On the other side, without settling it, it is often common for disputes to intensify and generate ill will. How do you boost the relationship's likelihood of a fruitful response to the disputes? To save your friendship, these are some of the most powerful tips:

Express what you feel but without accusing your partner:

Assumptions that attack the integrity of your wife explicitly may be highly detrimental to a partnership. If a man is irritated with the envy of his woman says you are utterly crazy, so he encourages her to get aggressive, and more discussion will be shut down. A more proactive solution is to use the assertions and combine them with examples of actions. Without criticizing your mate, rely on how you believe, and behavior explanations reflect on a single behavior your spouse is engaged in, instead of a character defect. These techniques are blunt but don't threaten the integrity of your spouse. It can, though, be remembered that, in certain cases, these overt negative approaches may be positive. Analysis has found that accusing and denying one's spouse during a disputed argument are correlated with poorer marital happiness over time for partners with comparatively mild difficulties and appeared to make difficulties worse. A new image arose for spouses with big issues. Immediately during the confrontation argument, accusing and dismissing actions culminated in less happiness, but the issues changed over the long run, contributing to improvements in partner happiness.

Be clear in conversations with your partner:

People often don't really come out and explicitly say what's worrying them, but rather prefer more subtle forms to convey their dissatisfaction. In a manner that is demeaning and suggests inherent animosity, one spouse can talk to the other. Other times, without even addressing a problem, couples may laze and pout. Partners can often clearly prevent addressing a subject by moving subjects easily as the dilemma occurs or by becoming untruthful. Such an informal manner of expressing frustration is not productive so they do not give a clear understanding of how to react to the individual who is the focus of the behavior. They realize their spouse is frustrated, but without instructions on what they should do to fix the dilemma, the lack of decisiveness affects them.

Don't say always or never:

You should stop making generalizations regarding your spouse while you are solving an issue. It is possible that comments such as "You constantly look at your mobile phone, or "You rarely work out at the home" would render your spouse defensive. This tactic is likely to cause your spouse to start creating alternative explanations of all the occasions they were, in reality, helpful or mindful, instead of initiating a conversation of how your spouse might be even more helpful or responsive. Again, you have no need to place your companion on the defense.

Listen carefully to your partner:

Feeling that your companion isn't paying much attention to you may be quite upsetting. You're not offering them an opportunity to articulate themselves as you disturb your companion or presume that you understand whatever they're saying. And if you're sure about understanding where your spouse comes from or understanding what they're trying to suggest, you could be mistaken, and your spouse might still sound like you are not interested. By incorporating constructive listening methods, you will reassure your companion that you are paying much attention. Summarize what they mean when your spouse says, i.e., rephrase it with your own terms. When they start, this can reduce the conflict. By making sure you are accurately reading the responses of your partner, you can even perception-check. You appear annoyed, for example, by the response, is it right? All these techniques reduce uncertainty and convey to your companion that you actually listen to them and think about what they suggest.

Manage your own battles:

You ought to stick to one topic at a time if you wish to hold a fruitful conversation. Unhappy partners are apt to pull several subjects, a habit-recognized dispute, called kitchen-sinking, into one conversation. This applies to anything but the sink, which means that all imaginable items have been used in the old phrase. This is definitely not the technique you carry with you when you try to fix personal issues. Imagine if you needed to learn about ways to integrate into your everyday life more physical activity. You do not decide that now will also be a perfect opportunity to learn about ways to accumulate some investment savings, organize your wardrobe, and find out how to cope with an uncomfortable job scenario. One at a time, you'll strive to address these issues. This sounds simple, but a struggle over one subject will transform into a moaning session in heat of the battle, with both spouses exchanging complaints. The more concerns you pose, the less probable it is that all of them can be addressed and answered in full.

Don't show resistance to the complaints of your partner:

It is hard not to feel defensive when you are criticized. Yet defensiveness is not a problem solver. Assume a couple fighting because the woman needs to do more work around the house for her spouse. As she advises him to do a fast clean-up before he gets able to leave mostly in the morning, he responds yeah, it will help, but in the early hours, he doesn't really have time. When she proposes that he put down any time mostly on weekends, he says yeah, this might be a way to set it, but they already have weekend activities, and he has a job to make progress on, so that's not going to work. This okay-butting conduct shows that it is not worth her feelings and opinions. Another harmful, protective conduct is inter-complaining, whenever you react with each of your own to your partner's argument. Responding to you, for instance, doesn't tidy up well in the home, with you becoming a neat freak. Hearing your spouse out and considering what they're thinking is vital.

Consider your time for having a time-out:

If you see yourself falling into negative behaviors and find that either you or your spouse are not following the tips above, actually take a time out from your debate. It should be enough for even a brief break for a few deep breaths to cool high tempers.

Avoid showing disdain or contempt for your partner:

Of all the negative things that you can do and say during a conflict, contempt might be the worst. It is the top predictor of divorce. Contemptuous comments are ones that belittle the mate. Sarcasm and name-calling can involve this. Nonverbal actions, such as rolling your eyes or smirking, may also be used. Such behavior is highly rude and suggests that your companion is disgusted with you. Getting a critique in it, this sort of disdain makes it difficult to participate in a serious conversation and is likely to provoke resentment from your spouse rather than an effort to fix the question.

Understanding different perspectives:

You ought to take that opinion to attempt and grasp where they are coming from, in order to listen to your mate. Those that can take the viewpoint of their partner are less frustrated during a debate about conflict. Some other study has shown that it can also be beneficial to take a much more objective viewpoint. Researchers conducted a straightforward intervention in marital quality, requesting respondents to report about such a particular dispute they used to have with their spouses from the point of view of an impartial third person who wished the best for the couple's two members. Three to four times a year, couples who enrolled within that twenty-minute writing task retained a steady rate of life adjustment over the span of each year, whereas couples who reported no decreases in dissatisfaction.

Don't get exhausted with negativity:

Not reacting to the bad behavior of a partner with even more poor behavior can be difficult. But it would only render the conflict harder to satisfy the impulse. As partners indulge in reciprocity with detrimental consequences, they exchange ever more heated criticisms and disdainful remarks. And the bitterness escalates as the debate goes on. But too much negativity is too much. The correct number is a ratio of 5 to 1: partners that preserved a rate of 5 positive attitudes for each unpleasant activity (e.g., efforts at good communication, cooperation, and warmth) were statistically also be separated or split 4 years later. How dispute analysis reveals is that both taking and handling your frustration from a viewpoint are crucial to resolving disputes well. It may be constructive for your partnership to voice your complaints, but disagreements should be skillfully handled otherwise you take the danger of making them harder.

4.6 Golden rules for a happy and long-lasting relationship

It's evident that as everyone's lifestyles grow and develop and then change with time, so will the partnerships inside them that stay consistent units. If you're lucky enough to have a life companion you develop and learn with, over your lifetime, you're expected to experience barriers, road hazards, and diversions, and maybe years along. So, it is important to know how to establish a bond during tough times. These transitions could include moving yourself away from sleepless hours out with mates become the rule in favor of waking up long nights looking for an infant, so from a loud and packed home to a peaceful empty nest for Ben. At certain points, they could perhaps contain weaving economic difficulties instead of organizing a luxury weekend getaway. They could be professional life-related, related to health, or related to grief, or both. Life can bring obstacles absolutely, so you can't tell for definite how certain obstacles can appear or will actually exercise a lot of influence over the consequences of them if any. But, learning how to build a bond that will survive the transitions is something you can strive for. Here are the powerful golden principles for remaining in a stable long-term companionship:

Say it out or communicate impressively:

It's called effective or pleasant contact, in other terms. It truly can't be the more enjoyable you've had to chat about difficult subjects, finances, commitment, faith, raising children, but it will be useful.

Behave with your manners:

"Thanks to you," "Please," and "always you're welcome," will go even a long way to ensuring to realize that you appreciate and value your companion and also don't hold him unimportant.

Doing some entertaining activities together:

Select a type of activity that both of you really enjoy (watching a movie doesn't really count) and render it a focus in the companionship. Discover anything you love doing it together: walking, hiking, and creating train sets, whatever else. The pair who play together will remain together.

Variety search is the spice of amazing life:

Restlessness will result in a partnership becoming unhappy. Trying anything different can be as easy as experiencing an exotic cafe or as exciting as a hiking trip to your dream destination. Innovations you build together will hold you feel connected to each other.

Fight, but in a right manner:

Bear in mind certain laws, which do not call the partner names, in attempt to provide constructive disputes. If things are particularly difficult, take a pause from the debate. Let some other entities complete his or her statements. While you're upset, don't start a conversation.

It's always better together:

Being in a partnership simply implies that you have created a union that you have not only exchanged properties but even acquired the concerns of the other. Tackle them collectively, rather than going at his issues as simply his own. There are two heads more than just one.

For e.g., if he loses weight instead of forcing him to eat on his own, enter a joint fitness schedule.

Share your choices and work mutually:

No one likes request, however, a consensus can be enjoyed by everyone. If you just want your partner to go and do something because you're not convinced he's going to be good, sweetening the offer is the easiest way to prevent a fight. For starters, if you bring her to watch the first film of her choosing, she will watch Tuesday night Basketball with you.

Little distance makes the heart of your partner grow faster and fonder:

Retain your separate friends and enjoy the night over without your important other sometimes. Not only does doing something without your companion cause you missing him or her, it keeps you sane, too. And if the friendship does not really work really out, you always have a mate of yours,

Learn to enjoy laughter genuinely as it is the best medicine:

Know how to smile at your own self. Since that is the greatest medicine, and at dumb errors. Trying to laugh it off is safer than being mad in the long term if he drops the $300 cashmere jumper in the dryer. It's just a cashmere jumper for $300, not really the ends of the planet.

Stop quitting on things easily:

Find a practice and, irrespective of matter what, hold it going. Select something which makes you always feel comfortable and keep to it, even though you're inclined to miss, if it's still telling one another great night, staying in as much as you would like once a month, trying to renew your marriage vows each year or sticking to have sex once per week.

Keep your perspective fixed on the goal:

Yeah, for the 10th time, he missed your colleague's name, but that certainly doesn't imply that he doesn't think for you. You are less apt to get caught up in any small irritation if you have your sights on the target and on the focus centered on the aim, being in a secure, working relationship. Note, all of you desire the exact same stuff.

Seeing healthy counseling or a therapy when it's needed:

Partners who pursue therapy through rocky times are more effective than those that don't in overcoming their problems. If the occasion arises, it gets tough to go to counseling. If it is from a faith figure, psychologist, or mental wellbeing specialist, it's as smart as ignoring installation by yourself and getting any plumber to bring in a fresh sink and find an expert and help work out strife.

Chapter 05: Strengthening relationships

The major approach of this chapter is to strengthen the existing relationship with your partner. Understanding someone you love who has anxiety and how to cooperate with them in time of anxiety is also discussed in this chapter. Ways and methods to recover communication with your partner and how to create healthy interdependence are all the aspects discussed in depth. Enhancing romantic relationships is the major focus among all.

5.1 How to strengthen an existing relationship with your partner?

If you've been with your spouse for 6 months or even have been committed to her or him for 5 years, out of shared love and effort, partnerships are formed by engagement and are

maintained. This will be an underestimate to suggest your relationship is special, and not trying to better it would be undesirable. Although each partnership is distinct, no one is perfect. You'll not only maintain a quality partnership with your spouse by doing all such healthier activities to strengthen your connexion, but you'll also demonstrate that you're willing to strive with one.

Focus on your own self:

For e.g., if you lack trust in your own self, you would search for affirmation in your partnership. How we feel regarding our own selves is exactly how we could behave in a companionship. It's important to have a good sense of self to discourage any toxic habits from arising with your spouse. Invest in some new hobby, and make your plans with a few friends, then take action to figure out who you really are as being a person. By getting in self-love, you would inevitably be the best version of your own for the individual that decides to fall in love with your own self.

Express what you actually want:

It helps to assess what you want, to obtain what you really want, and that's as true with love as it is with anything else. Know, it is really about what you desire, not about the demands of the community. When we search for the stuff we believe we can go for rather than the stuff that is fundamental to our individual personality, we get more and further removed from seeking real satisfaction. Begin by considering your requirements when it's about intimacy and setting up your goals in a relationship. What would you like to offer and what you really want a relationship to get out of? If you have a powerful hold on what you actually want, then you can realistically look at your own patterns of behavior to check if they are hurting or helping your quest for making love to stay and, if necessary, take action to make changes.

Ask for new things to your partner:

For every companionship, communication or interaction is the evaluating factor in success. It's good to wonder how your partner's day went, but when you wonder, again and again, it is dull. Enhance the discussion by throwing in the extra work to challenge the partner other about something more personal. You stop slipping into practice with this modified strategy and start having more substantive conversations.

Make your loneliness productive:

Whilst severe loneliness is not good and can lead to depression, from time to time it's normal to feel isolated, whether or not you are in an intimate relationship. And becoming distant from others emotionally doesn't have to be a drawback if you use

those isolated emotions as inspiration to make mandatory adjustments that can move your life in more beneficial directions. It takes effort to find an enduring companionship. When what you truly desire is something that lasts for a long time, you wouldn't want to opt for a sequence of superficial partnerships. Begin by giving greater care to the connexions you do have and trying to reconnect over time with individuals with whom you have lost contact. Make new connexions by joining or volunteering for specific interest groups and clubs. You never know if you're going to find anyone different, but once you go out there, you'll just find them.

Show your appreciation in a healthy way:

A relationship's comfort is the cause we prefer to disregard what our spouses do and instead regard their actions of goodness as our modes of hope. To say it simply, your spouse doesn't have to purchase your beloved ice cream or to fill your gas tank, she or he prefers to, and your understanding of this sort of effort can reinforce your spouse to be compassionate as well as remind you to be grateful.

Try to have equilibrium in your love budget:

Although kindness is generally deemed a good quality, with lavish expenditure on dinners and presents, you could be sending not the right message to an existing or future

companion. In reality, by demonstrating more of an ability to conserve capital, you will create a stronger impression because it demonstrates you are willing to practice control of yourself and are likely to gain bigger financial wealth over time. But when it relates to your money, be cautious not to look too rigid or too commanding. It might cause anyone to think that you're not fun and that the partnership won't carry anything in the way of enthusiasm.

Consider your date night at least monthly:

Among both your packed lives and endless duties, scheduling one night per month devoted to just doing exactly that's the very feasible way to assure that each one of you does have time and priority for one another. Irrespective of whether you like to change up your partnership or you want an experience that does not require Netflix, one night is the effort to go out on a date, however, the pleasure that emerges with it can linger even longer.

Get yourself into healthy talk:

If and then how partners connect, together with a personal desire to improve, dictates either or not conflicts may be addressed and hence the consistency of a partnership retained. With an affectionate and cooperative attitude that does not place anyone in a danger, certain issues, especially slight problems, are better resolved. Significant concerns will need to be discussed even more explicitly, however, this strategy is just effective if the two partners feel safe enough and confident even to react in a constructive manner in the companionship. If either or even both spouses lose that sort of trust, a defiant or critical response will bring much more damage to the partnership. To provide the most effective conversation, while you are providing counseling, you can still speak to the clients of yours regarding terms to use as well as light language and stop. Using terms such as 'I was wondering..., we should maybe... and how might you think about...' open up with the dialogue, whilst phrases such as 'You still..., you ought to..., you will never..., yet you can...' imply opinion, yet a dialogue would be automatically closed down.

Improve your schedule:

We mean, you're dependent on each other and don't prepare for anything (and you don't have to) to interrupt your life. Although you also have other responsibilities other than your partnership, contrasting all of your routines to see how it's feasible to spend a part of the time together is a nice gesture. Perhaps your partner will head to the fitness center a little early to catch the film screening that you planned to go and attend, or perhaps you can get up earlier to have your projects finished

so that you might make it to the central game of your partner. Though you should not have to risk your own life to please your mate, your willingness to negotiate should be as much enough to keep her or him satisfied.

Try to be open up when it comes to sex:

Usually, partners have varying degrees of appetite for sex and love, and they may experience multiple kinds of sex-related practices. Probably not unexpectedly, middle-aged people in same-sex partnerships appeared to have a better time than people in marriages known as heterosexual ones expressing their sex-related interests and addressing difficult problems with their husbands, making for a reasonable level of openness and continued trust in their companionships. Many couples who were able to maintain contact accessibly were often more likely to be focusing on their person and relationship problems with a well, defined aim of sustaining or reinvigorating their sexual relationships than such partners who had a rough time interacting with one another regarding sex.

Encourage partners to periodically arrange a time to have an eye on one another and discuss the well-being of the partnership like a successful therapist. It's essential to talk particularly regarding any and all facets of the partnership, involving sexuality. Knowing that there is a possibility for

dialogue will help ease some stress or worries that either spouse has regarding needs that are unmet and is also a way to remind one another that there is a respect for your companionship's wellbeing.

Let your past to go:

Whatever happens in your past doesn't always stay there as a perpetrator for many possible assertions and the innermost problem for future ones, and it's hard to go next in a companionship when you're still trying to think about what occurred in it in some other time.

And if you find your own self continuing to focus on the past, then it might be a sign of taking a moment to step yourself back and considering why are you less forgiving, naturally, or is something that you can't seem to forgive happening? You will find more transparency within yourself as well as what you do want from the connexion with your partner by concentrating on the rationale for this recurring feeling.

Stay high in a healthy manner:

While relationship desire and sexual pleasure will start to decline over age, partners who continue to enjoy affectionate, fulfilling sex not only express their sexual desires and have sex even more frequently but also integrate into their intimacy rituals a broader range of sexual actions. A crucial feature of equally satisfying your sex is mindfulness. It will help you to communicate your desires and feelings to your partner in a healthy manner by spending time keeping in contact with your body, with yourself, as well as your physical and emotional needs. Instead of thinking for the finale, staying in the present moment during sex can help you remain in touch with the needs of your partner as well.

Try to remember even the small things, as these matters too:

Another approach to keep the communication interesting is to genuinely listen to what the significant other tells, and chat about it in the coming time. If your spouse mentions a discussion with a manager that she or he wants to have, take note of your schedule and remember the day to ask about it. One that can touch her or him is the idea that you will go back to the subjects and specifics that your partner talked about. Overall, it's the little stuff that means the most, and there's no better way than initiating with your companionship to show this.

Respect your partner's differences:

You understand you're not really quiet because you are an introvert, but more, you're against small casual talk and don't like mindless tasks. You're more particular about how you invest your time and with whom you invest it than anyone, and that's all right. You may be searching for affection with an introvert fellow, but as always happens, if you are associated with an extrovert, accept and honor the distinctions and use them to the benefit (i.e. to make you try different things) instead of complaining over them. All of the good partnerships need rules, compromises, and the necessary giving into the distinct way of doing your things with a mate. Over time, a good friendship grows, but be careful of someone you believe is going too soon or too strongly. It can sound flattering, although it may be a sign of alarm that you are going in the wrong manner.

Express your affection to your partner:

Along with showing your appreciation to your mate, it is often recommended to display acts to demonstrate how much you feel for her or him. You know the way you feel regarding your mate, from taking your partner's hand at a diner to going for bed with one another at the end of your night, and she or he should must be able to observe that as well.

Try to involve positive psychology practically:

As the happy partners with their marriages have 5 times as many optimistic experiences as unpleasant ones. For a single good one, it might be not enough to attempt to create for a bad one, possibly because the effect of harmful actions is also far greater and broader. Express support for the spouse of yours at any moment, show appreciation, respond in a positive manner, overlook slights, and prepare to spend time while being together in complicated and engaging novel ways. Such investments in constructive thought and actions tend to build greater happiness in partnerships and will keep you back as you encounter potential challenges, disputes, and challenging times in your future. But if you are not in a companionship at present but want to be, be open towards new experiences at all times. Look up from just having an eye on your cellphone, take your earplugs out, and get involved with the world. Love is all around us and can be identified even in the interactions of every day that are seemingly unimportant.

Learn to apologize at the right time:

Being correct often isn't as critical as being caring. Although disputes can differ with your loved one, not every dispute is a competition to be won for. Don't get us incorrect, we're not asking you to bear all the responsibility, just to determine what fights are worth fighting over. While there is glory in thinking you're correct, during a dispute that is not as valuable as that person you are fighting with, there is wisdom in sacrificing and showing your apology.

Learn boundaries of your partner:

Does your companion, while she or he is angry, want to be left isolated? Will she or he mind that during the day you want to send a text? These questions are easy, but the responses to them would help you to understand and avoid you from breaching your partner's boundaries. Overall, the sense of confidentiality of your spouse is most definitely distinct from yours, so the only way to honor them is to realize his or her limits.

5.2 Understanding someone you love has anxiety

Confusing, uncertain, and intrusive is anxiety. It's challenging. Not just for those who have it, but also for those who value those who have anxiety in them. If you're one of those persons, you'd realize so well that the anxiety experience of the second-hand sounds terrible enough, you'd do any little thing to make things easier for the one who goes through it. If we deal with trust, anxiety, the appearance of the body, whatever it is, there is stuff we just need to make the environment a little better, a little more stable, and a little less terrifying. We've all got our list. If someone you love is anxious, their list will probably look a little something like this:

This is no biggie, so you don't have to behave like it is:

Nothing can make sense in the midst of an anxiety crisis, so it's better not to question what's happening or whether they're all right. They won't be all that. And at the seams, it can sound like the universe is crashing down. They will feel bad, so they would get through it. If you've already seen it all before, there won't be any need to ask, and they'll love that you don't know. Reassure, maybe somewhere private or more personal, whether they choose to go elsewhere. Don't get panic or do it to offer them the impression that you ought to look after them. Physical exercise is the normal end of the response named as fight or flight and is the pressure point for anxiety. You can go out with them for a walk. Only be there, otherwise. They'll realize what to do. They've seen that a number of times before. It'll happen eventually, because when it does, they'll be able to speak to you about what's happened, just wait a minute. Listen, then. All of us would appreciate it when somebody will just be there.

Do not confuse their desire for their world to be regulated with their desire to control you. They may look the same but they aren't:

The need to handle anything that could go wrong is a tough task. For the same motives that push nervous individuals to ensure that everybody gets everything they need for, everything is taken care for, things are also under control, and the risk of something going wrong is reduced, you might even feel monitored for the same purposes you're searching for. For what it is, see it. It's the desire to feel secure and in charge, not the desire to charge you, of the risk of anxiety controlling the stage. You could get upset, that's all right, and that goes across all partnerships. Having patience doesn't imply that you have to be ok with each and everything that's put next to you, but if you need to, chat it over gently. Don't, however, be critical. That nobody wants. Just note, though your opposition might look like a won't theirs, but look like a can't.

Actually, anxiety is physical:

As anxiety is an essentially natural physical reaction to a somewhat over-protective brain. It's not mad, and it's not frail. There is a rudimentary portion of the human brain that is oriented towards perceiving risk. It's just motion, not a lot of thinking patterns because it's in us all. It sparks up a lot earlier for certain persons and for a lot less intent than it is in others. It spikes your body with adrenaline and cortisol (which is a stress hormone) when it does, to have the body prepared to run for or fight for its life. This is the reaction to fight or flight and it's in us. It's just that the going tab is a bit more resilient for some people (those with anxiety).

With character or courage, anxiety has actually nothing to do with it. None at all:

Having courage is feeling yourself at the edge and pushing past it. We all have our boundaries, but persons with anxiety are more mindful of their limitations. Amid this, the things that press against their sides are continually standing up against them. That's bravery, and anxious people have it in loads. So reassure them that you see them really who they are and that this has little to do with what they often do with anxiety. People having anxiety are strong, and you have to deal with anything like that. They're sure that they're going to be as delicate to you and what you desire as they are to their culture. That makes them very amazing to be around. Anxious individuals would take the extra step to guarantee that there is a strategy and that everybody is secure, comfortable, and has what they need to control the potential of everything that sparks an attack. They are trustworthy. They are wise, they're thinkers (and that is what often gets in their way). They may be funny, caring, spirited, and courageous. So presume it's like this, they're no different than anyone else. The element that often trips them up (their anxiety), like with anyone, is often the element that raises them just above the crowd.

As members of your tribe, you'll like them. They are pretty wonderful to have around you:

Because of their desire to be healthy and ready for the next time fear raises its head, individuals who deal with fear will normally have a strategy, and they'll have worked tirelessly to ensure that it works not only for themselves but for everyone concerned. They're trying to make sure it's all coordinated to keep everybody safe, comfortable, on schedule, and stay out of trouble. They're there to make sure everybody gets everything they need, because if there's something they haven't thought about, then, that may not be worth worrying about. Notice that there's loads of interesting stuff they do. Let them realize that you value them regardless of who they are, not through it, even who they are while having anxiety.

Be sure that there's a place to tell no. And don't personally take it:

Plans can often need to be adjusted to stay clear of anxiety that falls in suddenly. People, who have anxiety (they're pretty awesome like that) would be receptive to the needs and shifting plans is not something they'll do lightly. We would never take your versatility for granted. In the world, there are a lot of things that most individuals think little about, but which may be the onset of an anxiety attack on a hyper-drive brain. Often, items that are vague or neutral may be interpreted as a danger, not by the individual, but by a brain that is overprotective. People having anxiety are super-conscious about all that does, including smells, people, noises, possibilities. When your mind is attracted to so many things, it is overwhelming. Don't personally take no one, they're never supposed that way. Remember that it doesn't imply they don't want to be with you simply because they do not want to continue doing what you're doing. Keep asking, and don't believe that anything you give will not be reached, but if you're not taken up on your give, be accommodating and not a big deal. They are responding no to a possible invasion of anxiety. And not to you.

Don't attempt to make sense of what is going on:

People with anxiety realize they don't make sense of their anxiety. It is what makes things so challenging. Explaining why there's nothing to care about is not going to prove much, it's only going to mean nothing, and they know this already. They must have convinced themselves that they shouldn't care a billion times the amount of times you convinced them. So far, if it hasn't helped, maybe another one won't make a great difference. Be understanding, cool, and comfortable, and really be there above all else. Anxiety sounds flighty and there's sometimes nothing easier than finding someone next to you

who is grounded, open, and all right to walk through this for you without wanting to change you. It is as successful to advise them not to be anxious as to ask you not to care about these pink elephants. Try not to even worry about pink elephants jumping out of a branch. In their heads, with roses. Only avoid wondering, about these mad huge pink babes. See if it operates that way.

What you need to do is get over it, says the guy who doesn't really get it:

As anxiety just occurs and there's always no real objective. So if you're saying that they really ought to get over it, the simple question is what to get over? They would have offered it to their own selves and gotten over it years before if people having anxiety just wanted a little motivation to get over it. Asking them to get over this is like asking them that they're doing something not right. You're not asking an asthmatic to simply relax. Hard affection is not affection. It is just rough. It's really not quite that.

Loads of affection have never damaged anybody:

Be empathetic and be there. Chat about the things regarding them that you enjoy. There would be occasions that individuals with anxiety believe like they are nervous and like they are a cause of the trouble. That didn't feel like they were making

things more complicated than they ought to be? So be truthful. In fact, when arrangements need to be modified, when you are in need to book a couple of rows back from the very front row, switch down the TV, take the long route, it's about when. If this is the hardest thing a mate has to contend with, sign up for it.

Don't threaten to get them changed:

You would like to offer suggestions. Don't, however. Let them realize that they're totally happy with you, the way they are and that you don't have to adjust or fix them. Then, of course, if they call for your help, go for it. Otherwise, let them realize that they are appropriate. Currently, more than enough. Just the way that they are.

5.3 Ways to recover communication with your partner

The greatest misunderstanding is about communicating is just the same as chatting or conversing on how to interact with your mate. At its heart, interaction in partnerships is about communicating and utilizing your mental, physical, and written talents to meet the needs of your spouse. It's not just casual talk creation. It's about getting the point of view of your partner, giving encouragement, and having your spouse feel you're their fan. Below are several powerful ways to teach you how you should interact in a safe way with your spouse:

Try to recognize your styles of communication:

You need to understand that not everybody has the same interaction habits until you focus on discovering ways to enhance interaction in a partnership. Some people want to chat, some like contact, while others are more tactile than an external explanation of feelings or react best to gift-giving. And you know which type of contact you want, but what really about your spouse? Relationships and communication are both separate. Good communication can come by knowing this for your mate. Your companion may be asking you just what they want, but you must be mindful of how this knowledge is conveyed to you. You'll lose the chance to create confidence and affection if there's a communication failure, and you'll both feel irritated.

Start seeing your companion react to multiple perceptive signals over one day or two while attempting to understand how to interact better. Does it appear like she or he reacts best to watching and seeing? Speaking of being heard? Or to contact and to do? For instance, having plenty of your eye contact and subtle facial gestures cannot convey as well to them as you assume if your spouse is more receptive to voice, tone as well as other auditory signals. You give signals, so they're not going to pick them up. On the other side, if you notice that you are an individual relying on auditory skill and that your spouse is a tactile individual, note that it will not be enough to claim that I love you. With the touch, affirm your affection, and continue to do so regularly.

Knowing if the needs of your partner are being satisfied:

There is one surest way to tell that if your partner in your partnership is having these 6 human needs met: pose the correct questions and further listen closely to the responses. Focus on what your companion said, and then inquire by repeating their argument and checking whether you understand right if you are not sure what she or he implies. The secret to how to engage in a partnership is sometimes not at least in the direct verbal contact, it's in the manner our spouse is spoken to. Your companion may be asking you just what the issue is, so if you don't listen, you're going to skip it. Avoid the lure of just waiting to end what they are talking with your companion before you can move into your turn. It's not listening, it's waiting for discussion. Alternatively, listen with a relaxed, clear mind to really understand what they are asking you. This would not just help you understand how to properly interact, but will also encourage you to engage on a deeper level with your spouse.

Try to be open and honest:

As about how to enhance intimacy in a partnership, being truthful and transparent must be at the list's top. Say what you actually mean, and make clear your emotions as well as your needs. It appears deceptively secure and relaxed to withdraw from confrontation, but it's no substitution for confidence in a partnership and it can never going to help you understand how to connect properly. Moving away from a situation is a partial method of coping with an unresolved dilemma of communication that can be used just to obtain a quick cooling-down time. You must be willing to believe that what you think will be understood and appreciated when you are not agree with your spouse, and your spouse will do so. You may catch yourself burying your feelings to appease one another and escape conflicts whether you or your spouse (or both) are averse to confrontation. A two-way companionship turns this partial peacekeeping aid giving band into a single-way street, and it is not a feasible outcome. It will eventually erode the satisfaction and affection you used to exchange, and it will also take the friendship with it. It's important that you both understand how to interact better with one another, instead of avoiding problems.

Try to make letting things go when it's useless to explore them:

Avoid causing a straightforward conversation about what's happening now to turn into a retread of any mistake involving you and your spouse that has ever occurred. In partnerships, this is the reverse of caring and productive contact. Instead, analyze the existing condition and define what you should do at this point. Pause to consider why you're here, to consider that improving the friendship, creating intimacy, and discovering how to connect effectively is the purpose, the result that you appreciate. There is literally nothing that any of you will do right now about the past, just let it go.

Other than doing the right words, it's about learning to connect effectively. You ought to be mindful of your own body language as well. You could give your partner all the caring and compassionate phrases in the universe, but your spouse is unlikely to react favorably if you have a frown on your face and your arms are folded over your chest. How to connect in a friendship involves listening for the entire being, supporting, and enjoying it. Lean into your companion, keep your face clear and calm, and stroke them in a gentle way. Show them that you are one of their amazing even though you are in dispute, through all of your words, expressions, and actions.

Be conscious in your relationship:

Be there to strengthen intimacy in partnerships and fully hear what your spouse says to you. Place time back to commit yourself to interact with your spouse 100 percent. They always can know like they have your total concern and that they really are your number one concern. When you're frustrated and depressed or are focused on tasks that take your time far away from your partnership, it's hard to listen and then be completely attentive, conscious, and mindful. This is a fact of life, but it is necessary to note that contact in partnerships is not a justification for neglecting it. Remember that when times are difficult, love, intimacy, and trust are constructed, not when they're easy. We will never advance and grow if we give up on any indication of opposition. Seize these chances to know how to cope with tension and pressure in a safe way and watch with your spouse as you develop and prosper.

Try to avoid negative patterns:

You realize what your spouse wants and you have talked of their favorite style of communicating, and there's something else that influences relationship communication that you are concerned about. Language specialists split down the way we communicate into tone, speed, rhythm, and timbre. Be aware and make deliberate attempts to modulate certain elements of your speech the next time you're in a dispute with your mate. An unnecessarily high-pitched voice seems defensive and childish. Often, it sounds like a query if you finish your sentence with a pitch of higher volume, don't do this because you're really posing a question, otherwise, you might instill in your partner fear. Peed just means how easily you speak. Take a deep breath, particularly when you disagree, and calm down. To bring the point through, talk softly and plainly.

Pay attention to noise and avoid fighting to be noticed, particularly noise creep, rivalry just contributes to miscommunication and yelling. Being louder won't help you and your spouse connection. You need to listen while your spouse is speaking. Timbre relates to the emotional consistency, mood, and sound of your speech. Pay attention to this carefully, and observe for red flag timbres such as sarcasm that can diminish relationship communication and cause mistrust between companions. Bending the pattern as things get out of control. In order to maintain the dialogue going in the right way, be playful, and use satire. Injecting laughter into the scenario will help things sound less dire and will deliver the two of you incredible outcomes. Since comedy allows you to restore perspective and equilibrium, it is an important component of healthy relationship contact. In your daily life, it often relieves the stress of you and increases your mental happiness. In this case, the greatest value of laughter is that it tells you that you enjoy just being with one another as partners. It teaches you that even though things sound difficult, you will appreciate your time together.

5.4 How to create healthy interdependence?

Most of us, particularly in our intimate relationships, respect interactions with others. In reality, we are designed for communication and it helps us to establish connexions with our spouse and to establish intimacy. Long-term partnership performance relies largely on the nature of our intimate companionship with one another. While we do think of our perfect partnerships, we always think of our most significant partner as a beautiful, close, lifetime friendship. That cozy, secure, long-lasting bond with anyone we already know has our long-lasting back? How can we create a friendship of that kind? A partnership that allows us the liberty to be our own selves that facilitates our progress and enables us to be flexible with one another? Comprehending the distinction between codependence and interdependence is one of the core elements.

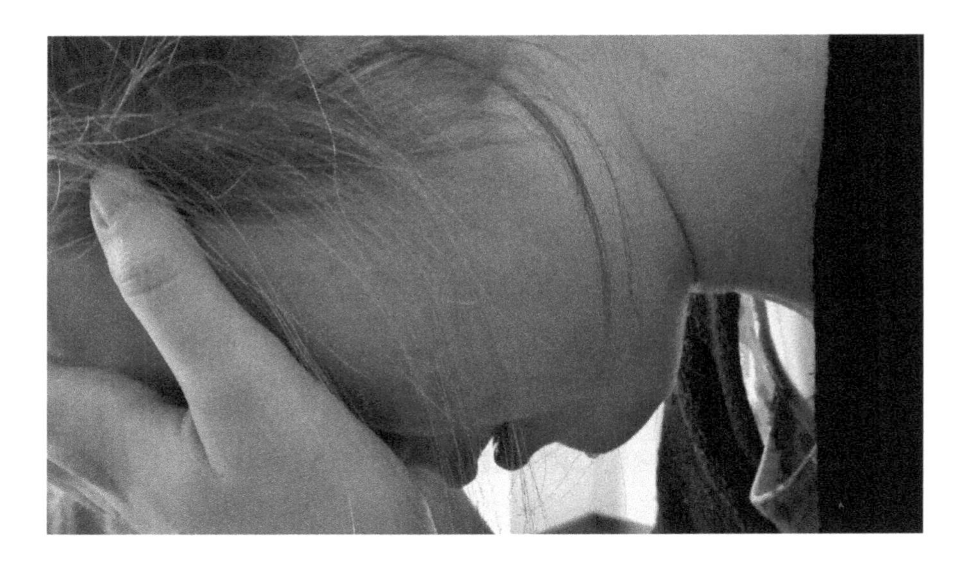

Understanding Interdependence:

Interdependence implies that the strength of the relational connexion they share is understood and respected by spouses while retaining a clear sense of self throughout the relational partnership. The importance of vulnerability is understood by a dependent person, being willing to switch to their spouse in positive ways to build relational intimacy. They often respect a sense of their own self that helps them to be themselves and their partner without losing who they actually are or their system of principles. It may sound frightening or even unhealthy to be reliant on some other person. While going younger, we are always given over-inflated importance of individuality, with a strong value put on not having anyone for emotional help, to be more self-contained. As vital as maintaining a sense of control is, and taken to an extent, this may potentially get into the way of even being able to communicate in a positive way with others emotionally. For those that have an exceptional sense of individuality, intimate interaction with a spouse may be challenging to attain, even terrifying or not perceived as especially valuable in a partnership.

Interdependence is healthy for a strong relationship:

Interdependence requires a compromise between oneself and those within the family, understanding that all parties are functioning in acceptable and substantive ways to be involved and fulfill the emotional and physical needs of each other.

Spouses are not demanding from each other and do not look for feelings of worth to their partner. In times of need and the opportunity to make these choices without the insecurity of what will further happen in the companionship, this gives every other partner space to retain a sense of self, space to swing towards each other.

There is a difference between interdependence and codependence:

The same concept as being codependent is not interdependence. A codependent human, for their well-being and sense of self, appears to depend primarily on others. There is little opportunity for the entity to discern where they stop and their spouse starts, there is an entrenched sense of obligation to another person to satisfy their needs and/or to feel okay with who they are with their spouse to satisfy all of their needs. A codependent relationship's traits contain items such as:

    - Poor / no thresholds
    - Tolerance

- No individual agendas or objectives outside the companionship
- People-pleasing attitudes
- Unhealthy, inefficient communication or contact
- Emotional relationship challenges
- Dominance
- Behavior management
- Poor self-esteem of either of the one partner or both
- Blaming one another

Codependent experiences are not safe and do not allow space for spouses to be themselves, to evolve, and to be independent. Either spouse or both, depend strongly on the other and the partnership for their sense of confidence, feelings of truthfulness, and general mental well-being are included in these dysfunctional partnerships. For either or both parties, there are always emotions of remorse and embarrassment when the partnership isn't going on.

Codependency involves the one who has dropped their core sense of self-image, so that something or someone external, including a person, a substance, or behavior, such as gambling or sex, revolves around her or his thinking and behavior.

Conclusion

There is more intimacy vulnerability and intimacy distress in individuals with poor self-esteem, which can discourage them from enjoying the rewards of a loving bond. Not only do individuals with poor self-esteem expect their spouse to view them in a stronger light than they perceive themselves, but they have difficulty even accepting their partner's claims in times of self-doubt. In comparison, acting out of our anxieties and insecurities will drive a spouse away, thereby forming a prophecy of self-fulfillment. Since this battle is internal and continues on much of the time, it is necessary to cope with our insecurities and also our fear, irrespective of situations, without distorting or pulling our spouse into them. By following these two important steps, we will achieve this; i.e. to confront the inner critic who sabotages our friendship and exposes the true source of our fear and anxiety. Like a near friendship, nothing awakens remote hurts. Perhaps than anything else, our partnerships churn up old sentiments from our history. In these cases, our minds are still flooded by the same neurochemistry. We all have working templates for relationships with powerful caretakers that were established throughout our early attachments. Our early patterns will influence our relationships with adults. Our type of connexion affects the people we pick and the complexities of our partnerships that play out. A stable pattern of connexion allows a person to feel more positive as well as self-assured. However, they might be more inclined to feel nervous and uncomfortable about their relationship if someone has an uncomfortable or concerned type of connexion. We get shaken up by partnerships. They question the core emotions we have for ourselves and expel us from security spaces that are long-lived. The intensity of our inner voice continues to ramp up and revive unanswered wounds from our experience. It is an invaluable strategy for getting to know our own selves, and eventually, for questioning habits that do not suit us or even align with our true, adult existence, as hard as it can sound to relate our current reactions with perceptions, values, and interactions from our early lives.

When we feel nervous or worried, looking at our companion to comfort us just contributes to more uncertainty. Know, these behaviors come from inside ourselves, and it won't matter how clever, worthy, sexy, or beautiful our spouse assures us we are, until we can conquer them inside ourselves. No matter what, within ourselves, we must keep striving to feel okay. This means fully recognizing the affection toward us that our partner directs. Everybody has anxiety, but by remaining honest to ourselves, we will improve our capacity for the

multiple ambiguities eventually posed by any partnership. Even when we know they have the potential to harm us, we may trust in a human. Holding one foot out of the door just stops the partnership from ever becoming as near as it can, and can also totally undermine it. We are bound to feel insecure as we encourage ourselves to be cherished and to feel caring, too, but holding it out has more benefits than we can think. The ideal scenario is that the friendship blossoms and the worst scenario is that we evolve inside ourselves as we take a gamble without allowing our insecurities to influence our actions. There is no lack of time that has told us much about ourselves or helped cultivate our desire to love and be open.

Lightning Source UK Ltd.
Milton Keynes UK
UKHW020650151220
375205UK00010B/471